UDL
University

UDL
University

Designing for Variability Across
the Postsecondary Curriculum

Edited by
Randy Laist, Dana Sheehan, *and* **Nicole Brewer**

Foreword by
Allison Posey, coauthor of *Unlearning: Changing
Your Beliefs and Your Classroom With UDL*

© 2022 CAST, Inc.

ISBN (paperback) 978-1-930583-85-6
ISBN (ebook) 978-1-930583-86-3
Library of Congress Control Number 2021949574

Cover, interior design, and composition by Happenstance Type-O-Rama

Published by:
CAST Professional Publishing
an imprint of CAST, Inc., Wakefield, Massachusetts, USA

For information about special discounts for bulk purchases, please email publishing@cast.org or visit www.cast.org.

Contents

Sciences

Humanities

Composition

Careers

Foreword

I n 2016, I arrived at Goodwin University (then Goodwin College) for the first time to conduct a UDL workshop. We discussed the theory behind Universal Design for Learning (UDL) and shared ideas for what implementation might look like at Goodwin. There was some optimism: UDL could be a unifying framework for teaching and learning across different programs. There were also some concerns: How would instructors have time to implement change with the busy year-round schedule? How could they maintain the rigor for students so they could enter the workforce? I left the day feeling exhilarated by the conversation but unsure of how UDL might take hold.

Since that visit, the Goodwin community has done a remarkable job of making UDL part of everyday practice. Professors have implemented UDL across many programs, including Nursing, Sociology, Histology, Computers, Math, English, and more. They have met regularly in professional learning communities to discuss teaching and learning strategies using UDL. They have shared instructional strategies as well as insights gleaned from student learning. Classrooms have been reconfigured and furnished to enable flexible teaching and learning environments. Professors have written blogs and have shared videos with the university community to highlight what they are doing in their classrooms. In addition, the university hosted a conference on UDL in higher education that showcased expertise from institutions across the United States. With time, UDL implementation has empowered both instructors and students at Goodwin for better teaching and learning.

Change is difficult without a vision of what that change might bring. In my book *Unlearning*, coauthor Katie Novak and I describe a cycle to support changes in teaching practice to be more equitable and inclusive. The Unlearning Cycle includes valuing variability, focusing on the learning goals, and prioritizing engagement and expert learning. The Goodwin UDL cohorts understand the importance of each of these steps. They support their educators to have job-embedded professional development. They value collaboration and flexibility in how each adult learner can build their background and take action. Their efforts are worth it; they continue to see positive changes in student engagement and learning outcomes—part of their vision for equitable learning at Goodwin.

The timing is right for this book. Educators are ready for a fresh paradigm for teaching—to go beyond the sit-and-get lectures and one-size-fits-all syllabi designed for a hypothetical "average" student. We know that our higher education institutions are not accessible or equitable for every student. UDL can help remedy that by enabling intentional design that supports physical, cognitive, and emotional access to learning. This book provides insights into how we can leverage UDL to move in that direction.

In this book, you will hear about UDL implementation from professors themselves—in their voices and from their unique perspectives. Importantly, you hear how design changes have impacted student learning. I imagine professional learning communities in higher education could use the examples from this book to spark ideas to implement in their unique settings.

I have enjoyed thinking of professors collaborating around design decisions that leverage UDL to support learning—to ultimately transform their systems and routines to meet the needs of every learner.

This book provides an opportunity to see what UDL looks like in practice. It offers inspiration about how small decisions we make in our classrooms can profoundly impact our students. For me, this book shows a path forward for equitable design in higher education with UDL. I am confident that it will inspire others. I am so grateful that these stories are shared. Congratulations, Goodwin University's UDL ambassadors.

—ALLISON POSEY
Coauthor (with Katie Novak) of *Unlearning: Changing Your Beliefs and Your Classroom With UDL*

About This Book

Dana Sheehan

This book started as an excuse to get together and talk about curriculum. Sounds dull, but there's more to it than that. Randy and I initially worked together on rebuilding a course during a Universal Design for Learning (UDL) professional development seminar, and it was fun; we laughed a lot. For me, it felt like I finally met a fellow professor who didn't think my pedagogical ideas were super weird. He had his own super-weird ideas too, and they were awesome. We were deep into UDL pedagogy and having a blast. Those meetings were what I thought every day at the office should be like. It was the exact opposite of dull. When the professional development seminar ended, so did our course rebuild, along with our meetings and our weekly laugh fests. We decided that we should write a book about these UDL adventures so we could "get the gang back together." In theory, we knew it was a great idea, but in actuality, it seemed like a whole lot of work. So, for a couple of years, whenever we'd see each other, one of us would say, "We really should write that book about UDL," and we'd never get any farther than that.

One day, Randy found me in the library, and as I was about to whisper our usual, "We should really write that book . . . ," he told me his idea to bring in a bunch of other professors to share their stories about their own UDL evolution. As we brainstormed, standing in the middle of the Goodwin University library, not being quiet and knowing we were minutes from getting yelled at, we both realized that this book shouldn't be only about UDL theory; it needed to be about what actually happened to the professors as well as to the students. We wanted to show the world what Universal Design for Learning truly looked like in a classroom. We also wanted to show both the successes and the failures, since the failures were essential in creating the future successes. We brought in Nicole and her share of super-weird ideas, and the initial thought blossomed into what you have before you. The gang is back.

This book is an anthology of professors' stories about their UDL paths, with examples of what UDL actually looks like in their college classrooms, both online and in person. We wanted this book to be more than just a list of ideas. We wanted to show how UDL works. If you don't know anything about Universal Design for Learning, it's OK. Basically, UDL is "a framework to improve and optimize teaching and learning for all people based on scientific insights into how humans learn" (CAST, 2018). Plainly put, it's a way to make sure that every learner has an equal opportunity to learn in a way that works for them.

Each professor discusses what UDL means to them. In their biographies, they talk about how they came into the world of academics and what drew them to UDL. In their chapters, they break down an issue or problem that had arisen in the classroom and describe how they worked through that issue using the Universal Design for Learning lens. We wanted to hear what worked and what didn't for these professors and what they themselves have learned through their experiences. One of our goals for this book is to give you a set of full stories about the ins and outs of Universal Design for Learning. So please settle in, read, laugh, enjoy, and hopefully, join our gang while you snag some super-weird ideas for your own classroom or department.

Introduction:
Accessing Higher Education

Randy Laist

When he explains the inspiration for Universal Design for Learning, David Rose will often show a picture of stone steps leading up to the entrance of a school. The very steps that are intended to provide access to the school building, Rose points out, act as a barrier for students who use a wheelchair or cane, as well as for other people trying to access the building with heavy bags or baby strollers, people on medication or people with asthma, and people in any number of foreseeable and unforeseeable circumstances. Building a ramp onto the side of the building can improve access, but it is also expensive, clumsy looking, and stigmatizing. The elegant architectural solution is obviously to design the building in a way that integrates both a ramp and a staircase into the design of the entryway, allowing individuals options for accessing the building in the way that makes the most sense to them.

Getting into the school building, however, Rose observes, is the relatively easy part. It is easy to see that universal design, a design that foregrounds accessibility for a wide variety of users, plays a critical role in the construction of physical spaces, but it is equally, if not more, important to apply the same principle to what happens inside the school building—to learning itself. In addition to accessible buildings, schools also need accessible instructional materials, lesson designs that anticipate learner diversity, and assessment methods that allow all students to express their unique perspectives. When we see a student in a wheelchair stranded at the bottom of a staircase, we are quick to hold the student blameless and criticize the building's designer. But when we see students stranded outside an educational framework that does not respond to their cognitive and psychological needs, we tend to place the blame on the student, accusing them of insufficient effort or perseverance. Inaccessibility in instructional design is harder to see than inaccessibility in architectural design, but it is just as much a violation of the democratic ideals that undergird the spirit of education.

Most contemporary college campuses have become models of universal design in architecture, with residential and academic buildings that feature ramps, automated doors, Braille signage, wheelchair-accessible lavatories, areas of refuge, and other design elements intended to enhance accessibility. In many ways, however, the "intellectual architecture" of higher education continues to present learners with obstacles. Higher education itself is our society's most highly valued "stairway to success." Earning a college degree is celebrated as the most common path to upward mobility, but as in Rose's analogy, college, the very thing that should be providing access—not only to information but to economic self-sufficiency, professional success, and personal self-actualization—too often confronts students with formidable barriers. While some of these barriers are financial, logistical, and social, they are also pedagogical. We are all familiar with the freshman lecture hall class where 200 students read assigned chapters from a textbook, attend weekly lectures, and take a common final exam. While some students may thrive in this kind of setting, it represents the antithesis of UDL, a model of education we might call "Exclusionary Design for Learning," a learning environment that seems intentionally "designed" to alienate potential learners and to sustain a traditional conception of the role of higher education as a bastion of social gatekeeping. Even in smaller classroom environments, the teacher-centered traditions of postsecondary education provide the default instructional method. While practitioners may simply be following the educational models encouraged by their department heads or teaching in ways that are consistent with their students' expectations and their own higher ed experiences, the effects of exclusionary design serve the purpose of suppressing social mobility, stigmatizing difference, and perpetuating systemic inequalities.

At their best, however, institutions of higher education provide exemplary models of UDL principles. The root of the word "universal" in UDL is the same as the root of the word "university"—both words express the aspiration to encompass an ever-expansive inclusivity. A college campus promises students a "buffet" of options for becoming engaged and pursuing their educational goals: different disciplines, different professors with different teaching styles, different classes and different kinds of classes (workshops, seminars, labs, service-learning opportunities, etc.), as well as, traditionally, a wealth of extracurricular and social opportunities. For many students who thrive in college, the freedom of being able to build their own college experience in a way that corresponds with their own learning goals becomes an initiation into self-hood that can be much more profound and impactful than anything they learn in their individual classes. For these reasons, UDL-based pedagogy fits perfectly with the spirit of higher education in its emphases on catering to a diverse population of students, teaching students to be reflective thinkers and master learners, and embracing innovative techniques and technologies. The language of UDL has been incorporated into higher education policy through, for example, the Higher Education Opportunity Act (2008) and the Strengthening Career and Technical Education for the 21st Century Act (2018); and a growing number of postsecondary institutions, including Boston College, the California State University system, Johns Hopkins, and McGill, all have UDL-informed initiatives on their campuses. Slowly but surely, the "UDL revolution" is redesigning what college classrooms look like, how college faculty teach, and how students engage with their postsecondary education.

Although UDL was originally pioneered in K–12 settings, the spirit of flexibility inherent in UDL theory allows it to encompass the diversity of postsecondary educational environments. UDL-informed teaching can address what CAST refers to as "the wide variability of learners in higher ed environments" (n.d.), but it also provides an educational philosophy that is adaptable enough to apply to the wide variety of disciplines typically offered on most college campuses, from traditional academic subjects such as sciences and liberal arts to professional studies in fields such as education, business, and manufacturing. While these diverse disciplines involve different kinds of skills, knowledge sets, and curricular regimens, UDL theory provides core principles that penetrate to the heart of any learning situation. UDL is therefore a powerful framework within which to reflect on course design and teaching practice in a cross-disciplinary way. Fostering conversations about how UDL principles apply in different ways to different disciplines can help to break down departmental silos, to encourage faculty dialogue, and to affirm a consistent institutional teaching philosophy.

Since 2018, Goodwin University has been partnering with CAST to incorporate UDL principles into our educational practice, as well as our organizational philosophy. Over the last few years, cohorts of faculty members have been immersed in UDL training, and many of the university's classes have been redesigned to anticipate and optimize learner variability. Throughout this process, we have fostered a campus-wide conversation about inclusivity in teaching and learning, and we have challenged ourselves to imagine how the principles of universal design can help us to reimagine higher education for today. Our experiences adapting Universal Design for Learning to different contexts have produced a rich repository of stories—ambitious experiments, inspirational successes, instructive failures—that dramatize what it looks like when UDL theory hits the "road" of individual encounters.

Meyer, Rose, and Gordon (2014) explain that

> The real world, with its messiness and complexity, is where we learn whether a theory actually works. In turn, what happens in practice shapes evolving theoretical concepts. As significant as the learning sciences are for UDL theory, practice is an essential source in the development of UDL. (p. 85)

Specific classroom encounters are the arena where UDL is put to the test, and they are also the experimental conditions under which UDL theory is refined and advanced. In *UDL University*, a spectrum of practitioners shares hands-on stories about how their UDL training has inspired them to redesign and reconceptualize the way they teach, the way they interact with students, and the way they think about the role of higher education in general. These first-person accounts of the transformative potential of a UDL-based approach to higher education offer specific examples of what UDL-informed practice looks like and practical strategies for implementing UDL-based techniques. While the focus of this book is on higher education, these stories provide educators at any level with practical illustrations of how to translate the theoretical architecture of

UDL into concrete lesson plans and curricular designs. While this book can profitably be read cover to cover to provide a total overview of the different ways that UDL principles can enhance postsecondary instruction, the chapters can also be read individually. Since each chapter approaches the topic from within a particular disciplinary context, readers can pick and choose the chapters that are most relevant to their interests and concerns.

Higher education, already in a period of intense disruption, has been jolted anew by the COVID-19 pandemic, which has required postsecondary educators to reexamine their approaches, their methods, and even their fundamental reason for being. While *UDL University* does not specifically focus on coronavirus-related concerns, it does provide a refreshing cornucopia of alternative approaches that can help to address some of the challenges associated with teaching in a time of disruption and transformation at the same time that it suggests broader solutions for reimagining the nature of educational engagement at the higher ed level. It is easy to see that the homogenized, teacher-centered method of instructional delivery is already long past its sell-by date. *UDL University* provides a vision of the varied and vibrant classroom dynamics that will take its place.

Sciences

Chapter 1

Kelli Goodkowsky

Making Connections in Teaching, Learning, and Life With Universal Design for Learning

Histology is the study of the microscopic structure of tissues. I became an instructor of histology after spending over 20 years supervising hospital laboratories. How did this experience translate into the classroom? I knew a great deal about the field of histology, but I knew very little about teaching. I was hired as a program director and content expert, with a teaching requirement. No problem. I knew my subject matter. How difficult could this be? Well, as it turns out, teaching is not as easy as our gifted teachers make it look. There is an art to teaching. Participating in a UDL professional development program transformed my teaching. I no longer feared my teaching or felt overwhelmed by it; instead, I was inspired to apply what I had learned.

One of the first issues we examined in the UDL program was the problem posed by various barriers to learning. A major concern that emerged from these discussions was the question of how to help students to make connections. I knew that students were working hard to memorize histologic concepts, that this effort was causing them great stress, and that this stress was creating a barrier to their learning. I also knew that being a histotechnician requires the laboratorian to work hands on with patient tissue specimens, requiring no room for error. Because there is a hands-on laboratory component to the program, students were deeply engaged in working with tissue specimens; the challenge was to further engage them in the lecture material by making connections to the hands-on laboratory work. For many students, training in the field of histology is similar to learning a new language. Connecting the lecture to the lab is critical so as not to overwhelm them. Although the didactic portion of the courses is separate from the laboratory component, I encourage students to view them as one. This has helped students to extend the knowledge gained from the lecture and directly apply it to the laboratory setting. One student enrolled in an introductory histology course commented on how viewing the lab and lecture as one is helping her to make vital connections in the area of troubleshooting.

Before tackling this challenge, however, it was necessary to address the stress that, for many students, constituted the most noticeable barrier to learning. UDL training helped me to arrange classroom experiences that asked students to connect their learning to their own life story, inviting them to work through the process of finding balance in their lives, in and out of the classroom. As I've mentioned, I have a passion for making connections. With one group of histology students, it was evident that personal and professional stresses were creating barriers in the classroom. Students admitted they felt stuck for various reasons when it came to connecting the lecture material to the lab. My challenge was to find a way to connect with them, where they were, without compromising the work we needed to accomplish. The best way, it turned out, to connect with this group of students was to take time during the last 15 or 20 minutes of class to engage in informal conversations about where they were and how their learning process was affected. The fact that the UDL classroom was equipped with café-vibe furniture was an added plus, as the relaxed atmosphere allowed for greater freedom to speak.

The informal communication time spent together proved to minimize fear and promote positive attitudes around the work students needed to accomplish to be successful histotechnicians. For example, sharing my real-world histology experience with students helped them to connect what they were learning in the course with how they might apply this knowledge in the field. This group of students further engaged in reflective practice at the conclusion of each weekly unit, a task that, prior to my exposure to Universal Design for Learning, might have seemed cumbersome given the amount of material students must learn. Although not a formal writing assignment, this reflective practice helped students to make connections between what they were learning and how they were feeling, identifying what they were doing well, where they could improve, and how they could integrate a balance of work and play as they moved through the program. Their reflections helped me to structure classes that were meaningful to them. At the start of each class, we took a couple of minutes so that students could share with their classmates what they did the previous week to promote balance in their lives. While reflecting on her current practice of retaining information (which she confessed was not working), one student was astounded at the transformation that occurred when she identified alternatives to her study practice. Taking a study break and playing with her dog helped clear one student's head so she could continue her work. Another student commented (to her surprise) that she actually enjoyed participating in group work because she picked up tips from her classmates for studying and retaining information. A key assignment for another student, a gifted artist, was the creation of a histology concept map. Being able to express her understanding of the course concepts through imagery rather than words proved to be the key to removing a tremendous barrier to her learning. In turn, her artistry provided her classmates with a visual representation of the course content that went beyond linear thinking. Laboratorians tend to be linear thinkers, and the nonlinear thinker in the field of histology offers a perspective that may be foreign for some in this field. The value of this out-of-the-box thinking, however, cannot be overstated.

Perhaps one of the most compelling projects I offered students was the #TeachMe Project. Several years ago, one of our advisory board members informed the group of a shortage of histology leaders. She reported that students were coming into the field highly skilled technically, yet with little interest in taking on leadership roles. As a result, a leadership component was added to the program, starting with one of the introductory courses and then reinforced throughout the program. The #TeachMe Project offers students the opportunity to take on leadership roles as they compose and deliver a presentation about any aspect (or an extension) of the course they are enrolled in and have an interest in further exploring. Students enrolled in a histology staining course worked as one team, with each student identifying their designated role in the project. The final project at the end of the course culminates in a presentation by the students to their instructor, along with a reflective summary that outlines their role in the project and what they learned. The assignment is scaffolded, and students are advised at the start of the project of how this project aligns with specific outcomes of the histology program. What I find compelling about this project is that it empowers students to take on team roles of their choosing, to make connections between course material and their expansive research, and to reflect on the entire process. Students have multiple options for presenting their project, although they may suggest other options for representing their work. Because most students are proficient at creating PowerPoint presentations, they must use a form of media other than PowerPoint.

The first group of students who participated in the #TeachMe Project represented their final research project in video format. They chose to record a presentation on immuno-histochemical markers for embryonal tumors, an expansion on basic immunohistochemical techniques they learned in the staining course. What impressed me about their choice of topic was their eagerness to expand on a technique, which, due to the pandemic, was only minimally touched upon in the lab that corresponds with this staining course. Because the field of histology relies on hands-on technique and the visual acuity of its technicians, preparing students to perform this work in a simulated laboratory environment is integral to their success. If this cannot occur, it is critical to find other means of representing concepts in order to make connections. Furthermore, many employers require certification as a histotechnician. The ability to connect histologic concepts with real-world histology helps students to pass their national certification exam. After reading the reflective comments from students about this project, it became evident to me that students were discovering their "why" of learning.

UDL is a framework that empowers students to achieve mastery while finding their inner motivation as learners. One student who participated in the #TeachMe Project worked in a hospital cytology laboratory. As he narrated the final video, connections between the research and his position in the laboratory became clearer. He commented that, early on in the project, he intentionally evaluated how he and his coworkers processed tissue specimens from the moment the specimen arrived in the laboratory to diagnosis. He noted that everyone on his team had a common goal, yet how they achieved that goal was somewhat different. This observation helped him to find parallels between his professional team and his student research team. He then interviewed two pathologists in the laboratory about their research on immunohistochemical techniques, and he described how much he learned about the role immunohistochemical markers played in diagnosing disease. The student further exuded confidence in recognizing his potential as a narrator and interviewer. Another student involved in this same project commented, "As a result of this project, I did gain a deeper understanding of IHC and how continual developments into diagnostic markers are helping patients." One of the most interesting reflections from a student was in the recognition of how telling a story and humanizing his team's topic helped him to connect with the research. When describing how he was going to represent his team's research, he commented, "I felt that just regurgitating information we found would be boring and not creative. So, I decided to mix in the story about Mary throughout the presentation to keep the viewer interested and to show how our information could connect to a person." He further commented, "I learned a great deal working on this project, from the complexities of group interactions to the knowledge found from research." The motivation for this student's learning was directly correlated with connecting the patient specimen to the patient, something we stress throughout the program.

Connecting with my why was integral to my success as an instructor. UDL extended my thought process beyond the parameters of procedural limitations and into the art of histology, with all of its fabulous intricacies. This newfound thought process directly confirmed for me that the instructor perspective and the student perspective are always connected. I have become convinced that the more deeply we reflect on the whys that inform the teacher-student relationship, the more we will be able to unlock one another's potential in the classroom and beyond.

How I Got Here

Kelli Goodkowsky

It seems that everywhere I turn I am inundated with messages that cause me to rethink what I am passionate about, to discover new passions, and to wake up latent potential. As a reflective practitioner, I discovered that teaching is so much more than the presentation of concepts. It is holistic. It is about helping students make connections to material in ways that make sense to them. Lately, I have been considering the many challenges involved in being a student, and I have been inspired by the degree to which Universal Design for Learning can help students to recognize their true potential. Universal Design for Learning offers an approach to teaching that results in greater student engagement and that unlocks students' potential, their potential to discover what motivates them to learn, as well as their potential for discovering new passions.

My passion is connecting. Perhaps because of my background in histologic science, my need to know why things happen often gets the best of me. I love investigating. I love the process of viewing the larger picture, breaking that picture down, and individualizing it in ways that create new connections. My engagement in Universal Design for Learning led me to bring my passion for analysis to bear on my own classroom practice, drawing my attention to what UDL nomenclature calls the "why" of learning. My chapter explores the power of Universal Design for Learning to activate student potential. UDL frees both the instructor and the student to think outside the box as they simultaneously explore creative ways to learn critical concepts.

I was not a career teacher. It became evident early on in my teaching career that the linear way of thinking that served me so well in the clinical environment would not necessarily serve my students well in the classroom. Universal Design for Learning provided me with the tools to balance the curiosity that motivated me as a learner and the passion that will continue to motivate me as an instructor.

Kelli received a bachelor of science in social work and a master's in education from Elms College in Massachusetts. She is the program director for histologic science at Goodwin University, and she has shared her pedagogical insights in conference presentations and blog posts that emphasize the importance to learning of qualities such as mindfulness and fearlessness.

Chapter 2

Amy Beauchemin

Curriculum Development at a UDL University: What Works, What Doesn't

After 10 years in business, I made a midcareer change to teaching. After earning a master's with a teaching certificate in business education, I joined the faculty at Goodwin University (Goodwin College at the time) as a course coordinator of computer applications. I taught classes, oversaw adjunct faculty, and revised curriculum. In the first few months as the course coordinator, I observed all of the instructors in order to familiarize myself with the course and the instructors. This was eye opening; I learned many creative ways to teach the course, but I also learned that every instructor was doing something different. I revised the entire course starting with the course description and student learning outcomes. Then I found a new book to use, increased the structure of the course by breaking it into four areas, and added formative assessments at the end of each section and a final exam. I also overhauled the curriculum of the course to ensure it was at the appropriate college level, increased consistency with the other courses in the program, and implemented a course-wide assessment process. This was my first experience developing curriculum and assessments. While I enjoyed it, I was unsure of my abilities. Once I received feedback from the students and instructors, I realized that the new course design had a positive impact on student outcomes. Maybe I had found my calling as an educator.

Over the course of my 10-year career in education, I have learned that assessing my curriculum regularly and identifying the elements that work and do not work are essential to student success. I am passionate about creating meaningful projects and assignments, and a part of that process involves continuing to learn new and innovative methods to engage students. In 2018, I was given the opportunity to learn about Universal Design for Learning. This was an opportunity to enhance my teaching skills and to learn new strategies for engaging students. UDL allowed me to see possibilities for students to demonstrate their learning. Students do not have to be limited to reading a textbook and taking a test or writing an essay; they could make a video, draw a comic, or sing a song. UDL provides more opportunities for students to learn in ways that best fit their strengths, and it gave me a way to see teaching and learning differently. UDL's emphasis on multiple means of engagement, representation, and expression helps me to be more creative with curriculum development and to focus on the what-ifs. What if we allow students to post a video for a discussion instead of a written response? What if we allow students to submit assignments in different formats? The what-ifs become limitless and spark innovation.

A few years ago, my role changed, and I started teaching sociology full time, specifically Introduction to Sociology.

Right before I started teaching sociology, the course was updated with a new textbook and an entirely new curriculum. As soon as I started teaching the course, both online and on ground, I struggled with the lack of detailed instructions provided to the students in the online environment. The online environment is quite different from seeing and working with students on campus; therefore, different supports need to be incorporated. Initially, I made subtle changes to support student learning by providing clarity to the course and the assignments.

For many of my students, Sociology 101 is one of the first college-level courses they take. Detailed instructions are needed so students do not get frustrated and "disappear." The course provided students with multiple means of learning the content, such as text chapters to read, PowerPoint lectures to view, videos to watch, and articles to look through. The goal was for students to select the option that worked best for them. However, that goal was not stated, and students thought they needed to read and watch everything, which was overwhelming for most of them. I added a statement during the first week of classes notifying students that they may select the option or options they felt worked best for them to learn the material. I also found that embedding directions on how to post to a discussion board or how to submit assignments was helpful. Another area I felt needed more clarity was the instructions on the assignments. I added additional details, such as specifying the number of posts required in the discussions and simplifying the language to help students better understand the directions and rubrics.

Eventually, I felt I needed to do more to make the course accessible to all of my students. I needed to figure out how to reduce confusion, increase engagement, and improve consistency. The course required students to read the text each week, complete an activity analyzing an article about a current event, and then share the information with the class. This routine was stable and predictable, but it made the course quite repetitive. There were also weekly quizzes for most chapters of the text, but there was not a quiz for all of the chapters, even though students were expected to read all of the chapters. During the last two weeks of the course, the focus shifted to a final project. This was a nice change to the curriculum and provided students with time to complete the project. Based on student feedback, however, the directions and language were confusing, and the rubric focused mainly on writing mechanics instead of sociological content. There were a few modifications I quickly made through the lens of the UDL principles:

- In line with the UDL principle of clarifying language and symbols, I revised the language throughout the course shell to increase student comprehension.

- I revised a variety of rubrics to ensure that the outcomes of the assignments and projects were clear. The revised rubric focused specifically on the content of the course and the course's student learning outcomes. This revision reflected the UDL principle of sustaining student effort and persistence by heightening the salience of goals and objectives.

- I added a second project to reduce the quantity of repetitive assignments, and I allowed students to demonstrate their ability to relate sociology to a topic they were passionate about. Each project included scaffolded opportunities for students to receive feedback as they developed their ideas, embodying the UDL principle of providing opportunities for self-regulation, self-assessment, and reflection.

■ To increase engagement, I changed the discussion topics to focus on subjects that students can relate to, such as race, gender differences, and social stratification. This revised emphasis was inspired by the UDL strategy of recruiting interest by optimizing relevance, value, and authenticity.

■ To increase consistency, I added quizzes for every chapter in the text so that students can demonstrate their knowledge of all of the topics addressed in the course. Additionally, the quizzes are open-book and allow students multiple attempts to master the material. This aligns with the UDL principle of providing options for sustaining effort and persistence.

After running the pilot, I found that these changes seemed to be well received by students. The students clearly enjoyed being able to have open discussions with their classmates about different topics and being able to select their own topics for both projects. I was pleased with the changes but knew more was needed. There were a few assignments that students mentioned unfavorably and a few assignments that did not allow students to demonstrate their learning as intended.

Ultimately, my goal was to provide students with a course that is consistent, easy to navigate, and rich with opportunities to learn in engaging and meaningful ways. To fully revise the curriculum, I looked through each week and made sure the directions were clear yet detailed. I updated the verbiage to be more accessible, such as by replacing the instructions to "read the text" with the option to "review the text." This change in wording provided students the ability to select their preferred method for learning the course content. Students who loved to read could select that option, and students who preferred watching a video could select that option. I looked at all of the assignments to ensure they related to the students. One of the projects required students to write an autobiography about how sociological concepts had impacted them personally. Allowing students to analyze their life experiences through the lens of sociology provides a deeper connection to the material, making the assignment meaningful and engaging.

The emphasis on relating sociological issues to students' own lives informed my development of an assignment that I created to reinforce the themes of the unit on gender and society. The assignment's directions are explained to students as follows:

Assignment

The assignment for the week focuses on gender, specifically how gender differences occur at a young age and whether those differences can impact people throughout their lives.

- Before you get started, you need to do a bit of research. Complete a quick internet search or watch commercials on TV to see how children's toys are advertised. Then think about your childhood and reflect on the toys you played with and the activities you participated in. If you have children, feel free to reflect on the toys and activities they interact with.

- Then create a reflection, either a Word document (1 page in length), a PPT (5 slides including the title), or a video (3 minutes), using the instructions and guiding questions below.

  - Explain what you observed on the internet or in the commercials for children's toys/activities. For example, what gender is targeted in commercials about cars and trucks or dolls? Are there specific colors, words, or sounds used for certain toys?

  - Reflect on your experience and think about how "gendered" the toys and activities available to you were. Do you remember gender expectations being conveyed through the approval or disapproval of your playtime choices?

❭ Express your general views on gender differences and expectations. Do you think parents treat sons and daughters differently? In what ways? How do sons and daughters typically respond to this treatment?

❭ Explain how "gendered" toys and activities have or have not impacted your life, mentally, emotionally, socially, and physically.

The responses from students about this assignment reflected their personal experiences. Being able to link their own lives to sociological discourse enhances their understanding of the subject and resonates with them long term.

Another assignment that students have consistently provided positive feedback about focused on the environment. The assignment requires students to watch a documentary on the damage plastic is doing to our environment. Then they complete a worksheet to analyze this sociological problem and identify a unique solution to the problem. This activity provides students with an opportunity to think critically about a current event. The students then participate in a discussion using what they learned about plastic waste. They need to explain if this information will cause them to change their opinions, recycling habits, and attitudes about who is responsible for plastic waste. After completing this assignment, many students stated that they were more aware of what they can and cannot recycle. Some students expressed interest in continuing to research the effects of plastics on the environment, specifically in sea life, and some started researching more on their own. Student feedback suggested that some questions on the initial worksheet were repetitive. The worksheet was revised to reduce repetition and to increase the focus on analyzing the issue.

The course also solicits student feedback in a reflection at the end of the course. This "exit" assignment asks students to reflect on what they learned and on whether their mindset changed because of what they learned. This reflection assignment also asks students to share any positive and negative reactions they had to the course. Overwhelmingly, the feedback to the changes were positive. The pilot for the course was very well received. Students reported that the weekly assignments increased their knowledge of sociological topics, that the discussion questions were engaging, and that the projects enabled them to relate sociology to their lives. Students also provided some suggestions to incorporate into future courses.

I am still working to make this course even more engaging to students. I want to update the quizzes so each chapter of the text is a separate quiz. I would like to update the PowerPoint lectures with narrated voice-overs to provide an additional option to learn the course content, and I plan to include short videos to provide an overview of what is happening each week. Ultimately, the Introduction to Sociology course started with a focus on the textbook and current events in sociology, but over the course of two semesters, the curriculum was modified to focus on engaging students in sociological thinking by gaining new knowledge and analyzing their lived experiences.

Universal Design for Learning has changed my perspective on student learning. While I have always strived to engage students and incorporate varied methods of instruction, UDL has given me the knowledge and the structure to be more confident trying new things. It also inspires me to be open to possibilities. For example, during the class I am currently teaching, I added an option to allow students to post an audio or video response to discussion questions instead of the standard written response.

Incorporating UDL strategies into course design can be time consuming, but I now see the benefits of providing students with multiple opportunities to connect with the course content, to receive information, and to express themselves. For me, this is a slow, evolving process. I make a few changes each semester to manage the additional time requirements of UDL, but ultimately, it makes a difference. UDL also provides me with a community of practitioners who are inspired by the vision of the framework. When working with other UDL practitioners, I am inspired by the openness to collaborative discussion focused on student learning. I draw inspiration from other instructors, and it enables me to develop new and innovative ideas for my courses—ideas that help me to meet students' constantly evolving needs.

How I Got Here

Amy Beauchemin

As a child, I saw my father go to work every morning. I did not know what he did, but I knew he worked in a big building with a lot of people. It was exciting when he would take me to the office. He had a big desk and a fancy leather chair, and his office was all glass so that he could see the people he supervised. There were also the holiday parties. I remember the thrill of walking among mountains of gifts separated by age and gender. I knew at a young age that I wanted to work in business in a big office building like my dad.

So that became my path: going to college and getting a degree in business. I worked in business for over 10 years, and I enjoyed many of the jobs that I had but never felt that I was going to advance to the level that I aspired to. Eventually, I was offered a position overseeing a location for a third-party logistics (3PL) company. This seemed like the opportunity I was looking for. The position required that I move to another state and make a failing 3PL location successful. I went, but I quickly realized that I was essentially set up to fail, and the experience was the catalyst that changed my life.

Through reflection and the guidance of family and friends, I realized that maybe teaching was a better path for me. I had always enjoyed making training manuals, and I thought training people was a good foundation to help me transition into teaching. After deciding to change careers, I opted to get my master's in education with a teaching certificate in business education. My plan was to teach business education courses in high school. Unfortunately (or fortunately), I was unable to find a high school teaching job, but I was offered a job at a local college. I was thrilled. Since starting at Goodwin in 2010, I have enjoyed being in the classroom and seeing the difference I can make in the lives of students.

Recently, I earned a doctorate in education, and I look forward to a long career in this field. While I do not have an office in a corporate environment with the fancy leather chair, I have gained something better. I found a career path that excites and motivates me. I am able to educate and inspire others so they can achieve their dreams. I have found my true calling: helping students learn through relatable and engaging curriculum while continuing to become an innovative and passionate educator. Although my dad is not here to see me achieve my new dreams, he would be proud that I found my bliss and my metaphorical fancy leather chair.

Amy received her bachelor of business administration (BBA) at Western Connecticut State University, her master of science in education (MSE) at the University of Bridgeport, and her doctorate of education (EdD) at the University of Hartford. When she's not hard at work revamping curriculum, her next UDL challenge is to learn more about the UDL framework to better understand the nuances of each guideline and continue to apply the framework to her courses to meet students' constantly evolving needs.

Chapter 3
Annjanette Bennar

Enhancing Engagement in the Technology Classroom With Nearpod

A t Goodwin University, I teach an introductory computer applications class covering computer hardware and software, Microsoft Word, Excel, and PowerPoint. When I'm not demonstrating how to use Microsoft Office, I teach technology concepts like computer components, internet safety, and social media. In the Computer Applications department, we had a common "introduction to computers" PowerPoint that we would use each semester to introduce the material. Every professor would attempt to have an interactive discussion while going through the presentation slides. One of the PowerPoints contained over 60 slides and was very lecture heavy. I dreaded every semester when it was time to teach that section of the course. As hard as I tried to spark engagement, it always seemed like I was the one doing all the talking. Because I was. The students' eyes always glazed over by the middle of the presentation. I always lost their interest and was never able to get it back for that unit.

One semester during my Universal Design for Learning training, I took the opportunity to reflect on my classroom practices. As I learned about UDL, the emphasis on student engagement struck me as particularly relevant to the dilemma of my text-heavy PowerPoint. I decided to consider multiple means of engagement to see what I could do to recruit student interest.

The UDL checkpoints provide the following suggestions:

- optimize individual choice and autonomy

- optimize relevance, value, and authenticity

- minimize threats and distractions

Through the UDL learning-structure lens, I reflected on my class practices, and I realized that it was not the students' fault they were not engaged; it was mine. The way I presented the material was the barrier, and I needed to change my methods if I wanted students to be more involved. I thought that if the lesson gave learners options, was more relevant to their lives, and minimized distractions, perhaps students would be more interested in the material.

The first thing I did to improve the unit was to break it up into multiple short minilessons. Sixty slides contain way too much material to cover in one class. I focused on grouping the material into common themes to be taught over a few class meetings. One lesson that I revised was a section about internet security. The topics in this lesson covered staying safe online, phishing scams, and the different types of malware. I wanted to find a more exciting way to engage the students in the lesson. I thought back to the UDL training, where we experimented with many different digital teaching tools. I decided to try out the app Nearpod. Nearpod claims to make every lesson interactive, and I was looking to incorporate an element that allowed for increased participation. Giving students the flexible option to use the app increased individual choice and autonomy while also providing new tools and supports to supplement the lesson plan. A benefit was that students could access Nearpod on a computer, tablet, or phone, which made it easily accessible for most learners and provided students a level of independence, since they could choose whichever method made them most comfortable.

Being a computer teacher, I was able to play around with the app and create my own Nearpod presentation without much difficulty. I uploaded the internet-security portion of the PowerPoint into a new Nearpod lesson.

To maintain students' attention, I incorporated questions that participants needed to answer during the lesson. To provide alternative options for assessing skills, I inserted an open-ended or multiple-choice question after every few slides. One of the first questions was "What are some potential risks to your online identity and your computer's safety?" I then instructed students to respond to the question by typing their answers into their device. Questions like these invited individual replies and self-reflection into the coursework, personalizing the task to the learners' lives. Ultimately, the inquiries highlighted the relevance of learning for students through this meaningful question-and-answer activity.

Since I had Nearpod open on the SMART Board, I could see the responses in real time. I chose to anonymize the answers, giving each student the option of whether they wanted to be identified as the author of their response. Even though there was also an option to display the students' names next to their comments, I felt that students would feel more comfortable answering the questions if they didn't have to put themselves out there. As the instructor, I could later pull the students' answers at the end of the lesson and link the responses to the respective names.

Another engaging feature on Nearpod was the ability to go on a virtual field trip. I thought a field trip sounded fun, so I looked through the available options and found one where we would visit a room that had a desk with a computer. The desk was messy, with coffee stains and papers, and there was an empty chair. The room looked dingy, with paint peeling from the beige walls. Since I wanted to incorporate this feature into the presentation, I told the class that this is what a hacker's workspace might look like. It was silly, but the students had a great time looking around and exploring. The goal of this adventure was to delve into a new technology and to try out an example of virtual reality.

Besides the field trips and questions, the students could go to websites within the confines of the presentation. I included a website where students could check the strength of their own password. Students could type their current password into the box, and the website would come back with how long it would take to crack the password. The time frames to break the password ranged from 6 seconds to 100 years. This provided an opportunity for the class to discuss what makes a strong password while showing them how secure their own passwords really were. I must admit that my passwords improved as well.

Other websites were interspersed into the Nearpod presentation. I made sure to include a question or an interactive website every two slides to keep the students engaged, and it worked. When I introduced Nearpod, the students were a little hesitant because it was new to them. Since we were in a computer lab, many participated on the classroom computers, and others used their phones to connect to the lesson. Immediately one student exclaimed, "This is so cool!" They were really enjoying looking around in the virtual field trip and having the ability to follow along. Each question asked during the presentation was followed by thoughtful responses and rich discussion. It was great to see the students so involved in the class and the topic.

An unintended benefit of Nearpod was the fact that students could see the screen and the materials in front of them. The computer classroom had multiple computers on desks, with a low-hanging SMART Board in the front of the room. Students who sat in the back of the classroom had a hard time seeing the board over the other computers, but with Nearpod, it was right in front of them. They could read and participate with ease, and it helped to maintain engagement throughout the whole lesson. The lesson was such a success that I wanted to learn more about incorporating Nearpod into other topics. I attended webinars, watched tutorial videos, and read about best practices. After a while, I applied to become a Nearpod Certified Educator and was accepted. I received a certificate that I proudly display on my desk.

Since my on-ground students were so engaged, I also decided to adapt Nearpod for my asynchronous class. I changed some of the slides and added more videos, since students would be going through the presentation without the benefit of an instructor leading the discussion. I changed the setting to be self-paced and posted the code for the students. I found that even the online students enjoyed it. The response from students was extremely positive. One student commented, "I thought it was cool and very creative and easy to view the slides." Another student described the experience by commenting, "Love it . . . it is a good way for me to learn a little better online." From the classes I surveyed throughout the semester, 87% of the students said they felt more engaged with the lesson.

Overall, I found the UDL-improved presentation to be a success. I optimized student choice and relevance through the revised lesson plan, and I created a safe space for learning to occur. I also varied the social demands for learning with individual, anonymous answers and open discussions, and through the application, I allowed learners to participate fully by elevating the students' level of engagement. Students who had been disinterested were now actively involved with the coursework. UDL continues to inspire me to find new ways for students to achieve success in my classes.

How I Got Here

Annjanette Bennar

When I was in college, I had no idea what I wanted to be when I grew up. My father told me a business degree of some sort would be helpful in many settings, so I went for a marketing degree. It was an interesting degree, but I wasn't overly excited about my prospects after college. I decided to plug away toward the degree and figure out what I wanted to do later. In the last year of my undergraduate classes, I began tutoring mathematics on the side to earn some extra money. I had so many students that when I wasn't in class, I would be tutoring. It was during that time I realized that I wanted to be a teacher.

Right after graduation, I landed my first job at an inner-city magnet high school, teaching business technology, while also teaching technology classes as an adjunct instructor at a local university. After a few years of adjuncting, I went to work in higher education full time and was able to continue teaching computer skills. For the past 15 years, I have been teaching Microsoft Office. I love being in the classroom, discussing technology, and helping students learn. It is very fulfilling to teach someone new computer skills or a shortcut that they did not know before. My favorite phrases during a lesson are "ohhh" and "ahhh." When I hear that, I know I have taught them something new.

The thrill of trying something new is why I love UDL. UDL has opened my eyes to a different way of thinking about how I can create an optimal learning environment to engage all learners. At a recent UDL conference, I heard a quote that resonated with me: "UDL is the way that we show students that we care." By making changes to reduce barriers in my own teaching, I am providing students with a pathway to choose how they can become successful, expert learners in the class.

Annjanette received a BA in marketing from Central Connecticut State University, an MEd from the University of New Haven, and a Sixth-Year Certificate in Educational Leadership from Central Connecticut State University. She began her career teaching computer applications in public high school but then moved into higher education. She can often be found promoting UDL to fellow cohorts of colleagues through the Goodwin University Institute for Learning Innovation. Her next UDL challenge is to rework the math curriculum to be more accessible for all students.

Chapter 4
Robin L. Young-Cournoyer

PechaKucha: An Effective Tool for Teaching, Engaging Students, and Supporting Success

Many students find Nursing 210, Families and the Wellness Continuum, to be difficult because it is broken into an obstetric and pediatric (pedi) component, each seven weeks long. Students must master extensive content in a short amount of time. This creates a challenge for both faculty and students. In order to promote retention, multiple means of representation have been implemented into the didactic portion of this class, including think-pair-share activities, active learning activities, an embedded librarian, open-ended questions, small group activities, math calculations, PowerPoints with fill-in questions, and handouts to complete during class.

These strategies were implemented over a three-year time span. I also utilize National Council Licensure Examination (NCLEX) review questions in clinical and class. The NCLEX is the national exam that students must pass in order to practice nursing. In preparation for the exam, we leverage the electronic testing platform provided by the Assessment Technology Institute (ATI) that enables students to log in and complete timed exams during Nursing 210. In this exam, students are unable to return to a previous question, which is in line with NCLEX formatting. The ATI final review session was offered at the end of the seven weeks on a Saturday or Sunday. Most of the students work full time, so typically only half of the students were able to attend such a session. In spite of all the UDL strategies we used, the average ATI final grade ranged from 78.9% to 84% from the spring of 2017 to spring of 2018. My challenge as a professor was finding a way for students to have a focused guide while still requiring them to learn on a macro level.

The UDL professional development program at Goodwin University introduced me to many types of interactive learning activities. One of my colleagues used the PechaKucha (PK) format for her presentation. This technique intrigued me as an effective format for creating a PowerPoint review for my students.

The PK PowerPoint concept has been in existence for many years. Originally it was used at an architectural conference in Japan to limit each presenter's time: 20 slides, 20 seconds each. It has since evolved, with conferences around the world adopting the PK method for presenters to pitch business models, making all their points in 6.67 minutes (20 slides, 20 seconds). This provides adequate time to present an idea and convey the key elements to the audience ("The Art of Concise Presentations," 2019), while also allowing the presentation to remain fast paced and concise. After conducting some research into the PK format, I created a PK review presentation for my class. I incorporated the PK PowerPoint into my class in the spring of 2018.

The Pilot

The "pure" form of a PK PowerPoint has one picture on each slide, without any audio portion. For my students, however, I wanted to enhance the density of the presentation as a way of encouraging students to make connections between different aspects of the course content. For this reason, each PK PowerPoint slide that I created for Nursing 210 consists of several pictures that correlate with key components of the class, as well as an audio voice-over that provides further detail on the subject matter. The same pictures are used in each weekly PK PowerPoint, so students see the visuals more than once to enhance learning. This PK PowerPoint provides an outline of how students should receive and retain information during this class.

The first step in creating a PK PowerPoint is to set up the template. Add 20 slides to the deck and set them to change every 20 seconds. The next step is to fill in content that is aligned with the class trajectory. When creating a PK Power-Point for the first time, I would recommend looking at your curriculum to determine where the biggest gap in learning exists. Where are the students struggling? Focus on that one topic and then create a review slide for that section. That should take about one to two hours. When you feel confident with this process, the next level is to utilize the PK formatting for class review. This may take up to 15 hours to complete. Introduce this PK PowerPoint to the students at the end of your class during the first week. Talk through the lecture as the PowerPoint scrolls through the slides. I strongly suggest you put the topics in the same order that they are presented each week in lecture. When that portion of the lecture is complete, reassure any overwhelmed students that it is normal to feel anxious, but they'll need to master the information by the end of the semester. They need to be engaged in their learning. Remind and encourage them to use this PowerPoint weekly. Post the PowerPoints on the course message board to enable the students to refer to these slides on a weekly basis as they review for the final. Also, it is perfectly acceptable to ask students by a show of hands who has viewed it and who has not. Peer pressure is a great motivator! The original purpose of the PK PowerPoint was for the entire course review, but students have told me that they have used it to prepare for their weekly assessments as well.

On the first and last day of class, students are shown a timed PowerPoint of 20 slides that change every 20 seconds. This format offers alternatives for both auditory and visual information. The students have the option of using "normal view," allowing them to listen to the audio portion at their own pace, or they may select "slide show," and the PowerPoint will advance automatically. Using this tool, students naturally make a quick self-assessment, determining which key points are critical concepts. The students are encouraged to utilize this tool as a review to guide their learning and promote retention. This enables them to self-evaluate and determine where their personal learning gaps exist and to create a plan to focus on specific areas of learning. It is essentially designed as a "scavenger hunt" for learning, and the pictures and audio clips greatly enhance students' ability to master the material. On each slide there is an audio portion that poses questions that require the students to locate answers in their notes, in the weekly PowerPoints, or in their book. The students are not given the answers to potential exam questions but instead are asked questions they need to think critically about. This ensures they are active participants in their learning. Once they have answered all of the questions, they can verify their mastery by reviewing certain slides again. Some students will create their own outline, become part of a study group, or create their own PK PowerPoint to guide their learning.

For example, one slide from a pediatric class contains four pictures. The first picture is of a woman who has anorexia, and the audio portion asks the student what symptoms a patient with anorexia would exhibit. The second picture is of a child eating paint. The audio asks, "What are symptoms of lead poisoning, and what would the different treatments be for various lead levels as recommended by the Centers for Disease Control (CDC)?" Next, the slide presents the words "We Love Math." This reinforces how important it is for nurses to know basic math. It is crucial in pediatrics to regularly calculate the safe dose range (SDR). How is the calculation of SDR performed? The last picture on the slide is of a person drinking gasoline. What would the nursing priority be if a child drank gasoline? Why? Most of the audio portions have more than one question for the students to think about and to connect with the pediatric material. When activated, the audio enables the student to hear certain key points about each condition, along with questions about that condition for them to answer to be better prepared for both the weekly and final summative assessments.

After Implementation

The ATI final is the summative assessment used in Nursing 210 to test the students' comprehension of the material. It is an electronic standardized exam created by the professor using questions from a test bank. The exam is administered in a proctored setting on the last day of each session's class. (There are typically two sessions per season—spring, fall, and summer.) The ATI results have been tracked since the implementation of PK and continue presently. The first time this ATI final was administered, the average mark in the first session of spring 2017 was 78.9%. In the first spring session of 2018, the average was 81.8%. After the implementation of PK, the ATI final results increased to 85.2% for the second spring session of 2018 and remained steady at 87% for the summer of 2018, fall of 2018, and spring of 2019. A survey was left outside the final room for the students to voluntarily complete to comment on how helpful they felt the PK PowerPoints were in assisting them in preparing for the final. The survey asked how many hours they spent on the PK PowerPoint, what grade they earned on the final, and how they would rank the usefulness of the PK PowerPoint review, from "none" to "very helpful." This was done for two years, and 90% of students who completed the survey felt this learning style was "very helpful."

Innovation and Diffusion

Since the creation of the PK PowerPoint in Nursing 210, both nursing students and faculty have adopted this strategy and used it to enhance knowledge and promote retention. Students documented in emails how they used the PowerPoints to enhance their learning.

> *I felt the PowerPoints made me want to pre-read and answer all the questions before class more than in the three prior classes. It was like a scavenger hunt for my benefit and allowed me to really grasp the concepts better. I was much more engaged in this class, more than in the past three semesters during lecture and felt there was a solid understanding of the material. It all came together for me. (A. Smith, personal communication, May 1, 2018)*

As A. Smith was getting ready to take her ATI final, I noticed that she had notes in front of her that I presumed were the

PK PowerPoints that I had created. When I looked closer and communicated with her, I realized that she had created her own PowerPoints with pictures that were actually better than mine. This is the moment that every educator wishes to observe: when a student takes ownership of their learning and makes it their own. As educators, we introduce instruments to our students in hopes of enhancing their learning. Sometimes the students embrace it and sometimes there is pushback. A. Smith and I have presented at several conferences across the country, which has provided educators with a direct line to the student perspective.

Another student email reads as follows:

> I attached a Word document that I made when we studied for the pedi final using the "Pikachu!" We created the guide as a group and brainstormed for each slide/picture. We went back to lecture notes and also the book and decided what we thought were the most pertinent things to know for each. We then transferred each one onto Quizlet electronic flashcards to study later on our own. You're also allowed to add pictures onto the Quizlet flashcards. We added the pictures from Pikachu onto the front of the card with the main topic and on the back side we had the pertinent things to know. (S. Jones, personal communication, June 2018)

Since the implementation of the PK review PowerPoint, four of the six full-time course coordinators are currently using some form of this technique in their classrooms to enhance learning. This UDL format has positively impacted students, other nursing faculty, and members of the greater college community. Additionally, through both podium and poster presentations throughout the country, we have introduced other faculty nationwide to this concept. This active learning instrument has enabled students to attain better performance results on their current summative assessments and, hopefully, to attain better scores on their NCLEX as well.

When we are children, there are certain activities that make us happy. In navigating our world, we naturally gravitate toward what we find most interesting, be it music, math, writing, sports, education, entertainment, etc. These childhood enthusiasms assist us in preparing for adulthood. If we are able to incorporate those skills into our adult life, we become more passionate, happier, and more fully immersed in our profession. Our profession becomes a fun adventure instead of a laborious task if we are able to implement the skills we have developed over the years. Each student absorbs knowledge in a different manner. In order for them to achieve their full potential as learners and to be successful, they must feel both curious and confident. The PK PowerPoint activity is one strategy that helps students to reflect on their own learning and to practice techniques that enable them to master difficult material and enhance their own sense of self-efficacy.

How I Got Here

Robin L. Young-Cournoyer

When I was a young child, one of my favorite activities was playing in my parents' basement, which served the purpose of both a general store and "community school." A pipe holder served as the cash register. I also had a mobile ice cream stand that consisted of a tricycle. I pedaled around the "village" selling ice cream. As children, we were given permission to let our imaginations run wild, and it was possible to own a store, teach full time, be an orphan, and run an ice cream stand, all from the safety of home. As I grew older, the dreams that I was passionate about as a child remained. I strived to create a solvent business and to teach. In college, I considered becoming a teacher, but in 1977, when teachers were graduating, they were having a hard time finding jobs. The practical side of me felt I needed to pursue a career that had more of a guarantee at the end of the four years. Thus, nursing was where I focused my energies, and after I received my nursing degree in 1981, I could have chosen to work anywhere in the country and land a job within 24 hours. Opportunities were plentiful, as there was a nursing shortage.

When I graduated from college, I immediately enrolled in graduate school to get a teaching degree, but then marriage, children, and life all happened, and my priorities turned toward my family. During my nursing career I always sought out opportunities to teach and mentor. I have always had the aspiration to learn as much as possible as well as the eagerness to share that knowledge. I found high school easy but college very challenging. The skills that enabled me to be successful in high school did not seem effective in college. I always felt there was a better way to teach, and I vowed that I would return to academia with the goal of connecting with students that struggled and helping them find the learning strategies that worked for them.

When I turned 50, the youngest of our three boys entered college. At this point, I reentered academia after a mere 29-year hiatus to pursue the degree that would enable me to complete my dream of becoming a nursing professor. That passion for teaching never left me. It took me 34 years to earn my master's, and it was well worth the four hours of nightly sleep I was granted for five years. I still remember the first time a student called me Professor Cournoyer. It was so exhilarating, and I was thrilled beyond belief.

After earning my master's degree, I became a professor at Goodwin University, which allowed me to work with a diverse group of students. I had been a nurse for many years, but upon entering academia, I was a novice. I attended numerous conferences in an attempt to implement techniques in my classroom that veteran educators were utilizing successfully. I struggled to figure out how to provide the most important information to students in an understandable and fun manner that would encourage them to think and to fully immerse themselves in the course content.

I am always seeking innovative learning opportunities to enhance the education of my students, so in 2018, I was selected to participate in Goodwin's UDL professional development program. This program provided me with the opportunity to learn innovative strategies to be utilized in the classroom and clinical setting. I wanted to develop instructional materials in a format that would allow students to learn at their own pace and that would guide them to success in my course. These goals inspired the development of the PechaKucha review PowerPoint. The "community school" I taught as a child consisted of children from first grade through high school. My "students" were all at different levels. Now as a professor, I understand the importance of offering multiple kinds of learning opportunities for students.

Robin received her BSN from Saint Anselm College and her master of science in nursing from the University of Connecticut. She has delivered presentations on her work with PechaKucha at the annual Nursing Education Accreditation Conference and elsewhere, and her latest UDL challenge has been to revise interactive group learning sessions. These interactive sessions had originally been created for an on-ground classroom, and her challenge has been translating them into engaging break-out Zoom sessions.

Humanities

Chapter 5

Ellen Swider

Personalizing Communication: Using UDL Ideas to Breathe New Life Into Asynchronous Discussion Boards

The signature course in the Communications department is Interpersonal Communications. This course
investigates various communications theories, with
a special emphasis on interpersonal relationships and how
individuals navigate them. Online courses have become
especially popular in the past few years and even more so
with the advent of the novel coronavirus. This means that
most of the students who take Interpersonal Communications choose to do so in an online and often asynchronous
format. Online and particularly asynchronous classes rely
heavily on weekly discussion boards to facilitate student

interaction. Unfortunately, this discussion is often inauthentic and a poor substitute for in-person discourse. Students often start strong and write in-depth posts and refer to theories from the textbook, but over time, they may lose interest, post less often to the discussion board, or submit less thoughtful and relevant posts. The death of a discussion board is the dreaded "I agree with your post" response. I too, as an instructor, am guilty of growing bored with discussion boards, and I often find that I do not post as regularly as I should or monitor the conversation as carefully. However, as the popularity of and demand for online learning increase, it seems unlikely that the discussion board will be retired, and so it remains: a pitiful attempt at replicating in-person conversation. Eventually, the discussion board devolves into something that is merely another task and almost never an actual discussion. It becomes a lost opportunity for everyone.

A second prevalent concern in Interpersonal Communications is acute glossophobia, the fear of public speaking. Nearly everyone has some experience with speech anxiety, and those students preparing their midterm speeches are no exception. For some students, this fear is so strong that they choose not to complete the assignment, opting to receive a lower grade for the class instead of delivering an oral presentation.

My efforts to improve the meaningfulness of the discussion board encompassed three goals. My first goal was to better engage students in the course material and the required discussion boards. To meet this goal, I employed the UDL emphasis on engagement and, specifically, the challenge of recruiting students' interest. My experiences have taught me that the opportunity to connect learning with real-world goals is very attractive to students, particularly when these are career-minded goals. I wanted students to value the discussion boards as a chance to explore the curriculum and to recognize the impact that interpersonal communication has on their individual success. This personal, metacognitive focus would make students' contributions to the discussion boards more meaningful and relevant and keep them (and me!) better engaged, while also boosting participation.

My second goal was to give students an opportunity to practice their public speaking in a low-stakes environment and to be able to see and reflect upon their presentations and abilities over time. This strategy would provide students with options for self-regulation. Students needed more opportunities not only to practice but also to be able to see and critique themselves afterward.

Finally, my personal experiences with education have impressed upon me the importance of facilitating comprehension. I wanted my students to see the big picture and fully understand how interpersonal communication impacts their daily lives, the other courses they take, and ultimately, their career goals. My experiences as a middle school social studies teacher and now as a college professor of communications have shown me how much better students understand when they can tie their learning into prior knowledge and real-world experiences. The field of communications is universally applicable to the individual experience. Everyone has some sort of experience with communicating and with the different theories that we study in class. By capitalizing on the UDL emphasis on activating background knowledge, I can better facilitate this new learning for my students.

I found the perfect strategy for achieving all three of my goals by reimagining the course discussion boards using Flipgrid. Flipgrid is like an educational version of TikTok, where students can respond to a prompt by creating a short video answer. Then, they view other participants' videos and post a response, either with another video or in writing.

Before each week begins, I log into Flipgrid with my free educator account and create a discussion topic relevant to that week's curriculum. I first write a prompt referring to the current unit and posing a question or challenge to my students. I can enhance my post by including some sort of relevant media, like a video, an image, a GIF, an emoji, or another attachment. I can also incorporate a number of other educational apps, including Google, Kahoot!, and Nearpod. As I am building the weekly topic, I can select from a number of moderator controls, too. Flipgrid's Topic Moderation feature gives me the opportunity to control when my students see their classmates' videos, either before or after they post their own videos. I can also control what sort of comments my students post, video or written, and the duration of each video, up to 10 minutes. I prefer to keep all videos to a reasonable minute and a half. Finally, I can turn on closed captioning for all videos and select the language to caption in. I find this option especially helpful for all students. These are some of the most basic moderator controls, but there are many others to choose from as well, including dates, notifications, feedback, rubrics, and video enhancements such as frames and filters. Finally, I copy the prompt and relevant media into the course learning management system (LMS), so that students can easily access it. Flipgrid offers participants a number of different ways to access each topic. I prefer to post both a direct link and a QR code to the weekly topic in the LMS. This gives my students the option to access the topic using their computers or their mobile devices. At the start of each new week, the discussion board goes live, and my students begin to participate in it.

As I have incorporated Flipgrid into my classes, I have run into the occasional objection. Although my goal is to facilitate public speaking practice, I have had the occasional student complain that they do not feel comfortable recording themselves and sharing the video with the class. While this is problematic because the midterm presentation is a recorded speech, I do give them the option to either record their responses to the prompt (the preferred method) or post a written response to the topic. Another challenge when incorporating video discussion boards into an online class is the possibility that some students will be using devices that do not support the app; the most common technical obstacle is the lack of a working webcam. As this activity is part of an asynchronous online class, my students are expected to at least be able to connect to the LMS and the course-specific software; a working webcam is not necessarily a requirement to be successful in the class. In these instances, most students opt to use their mobile devices, but others have gone to the library to borrow devices.

For the most part, however, I have received positive feedback from my students. Students appreciate the chance to see and interact with each other. The people on the other end of the computer appear more real, and the chance to participate in class through audio-visual media is novel. More importantly, my students can see and measure their success in public speaking, and over time, this format helps to build their confidence.

I recently asked a few students to give me their perspective on using Flipgrid for our class discussions and was pleased to get some very positive responses.

On the power of feedback:

> I would say the biggest thing that I've taken from this class is receiving feedback from others. It's something that I've always struggled with, hearing something that I either wasn't ready to hear or didn't want to hear at all. During our weekly discussion posts, I would get feedback from my classmates on what I discussed about my life, and it got easier and easier every week.

On the value of a sense of community:

> *I'm glad that we communicated via videos for our discussion posts because it was easier to get a better connection with my classmates.*

On the development of new skills:

> *I personally have a challenging time talking to a group of people and especially since it is online, I have a lot of anxiety recording myself and talking to a camera because I am camera shy, but then again, actually getting the chance to do our discussions in this exact way has helped me overcome this and it is making it a bit easier on me.*

On personal growth:

> *A big way I've seen growth in myself this semester is definitely through our discussion board. I'm happy that we are able to record our responses weekly because as the weeks go on, I can see how much more comfortable I get with speaking publicly. While it might not be the exact same as getting up in front of an audience and speaking, it's a step closer. It's something that I was nervous about in the beginning, but now I don't even think about it.*
>
> ———
>
> *This discussion post method really forced me to be proud and supportive of what I was presenting. You cannot hide behind a keyboard and remain in the shadows when communicating this way.*

As an educator, I have been very pleased with my decision to incorporate Flipgrid into my course's discussion boards. This enhanced format has allowed me to achieve all three of my UDL-inspired goals for the class, helping me to engage students more meaningfully, to provide them with authentic opportunities to practice and self-regulate, and to encourage the activation of their own background knowledge. Moreover, I have found that most of my students are already active on social media and so the move to incorporating Flipgrid into the class is not a big leap for them. Additionally, they appreciate the fact that I can create and control who has access to the weekly topic; there is no need for them to create a new login. It is helpful to download the app to a mobile device to record a video, but even then, students don't have to create an account. And once the semester is over, they can delete the app.

I also recognize that my students are often inundated with responsibilities beyond their schoolwork. A significant percentage of the students I teach are nontraditional and are balancing their education with full-time work and family responsibilities. The opportunity to complete an assignment quickly and securely on their mobile devices is both convenient and attractive.

As an instructor, I find that I too am much better engaged with Flipgrid discussion boards. It is not difficult for me to create discussion topics in Flipgrid and requires only a little more effort than simply building a discussion board in the LMS. I can also reuse topics from semester to semester by creating Groups. But, more importantly, as I find myself grading the same discussion board semester after semester, I enjoy the opportunity to interact more fully with my students. The Flipgrid format allows students the opportunity to articulate their answers and share their interpretations in a much more authentic way than a traditional discussion board. Each discussion board is fresh and exciting because it includes different people and stories. I know that even if my students are commenting on the same prompt, they will each have a different perspective. The use of Flipgrid in our discussion board ensures that this perspective will be unique and authentic to each student. This keeps me better engaged too and helps me ensure that I am a better teacher for them.

As I write this chapter, I am preparing for the next semester and a new group of online students. As I explore the chance to incorporate other mobile apps into my courses, I can see unlimited potential. I have already determined that I will incorporate more Flipgrid assignments into the course, but I am designing more sophisticated activities. Nonverbal communication in particular is a fascinating aspect of communications, but in an online asynchronous course, it is very difficult to effectively explore. When I teach this unit in person, I challenge my students to find and identify nonverbal communication in pictures. We share an image or short video to the SMART Board and then, as a class, analyze it. What are the types of nonverbal communication that we are witnessing? What intended and unintended messages are being communicated? Is this communication effective?

Up until now, this experience has been lost on my asynchronous online classes; however, with the guidance of UDL and the technology of Flipgrid, I can incorporate this activity (and several others) fully into my online class by challenging students to use Flipgrid to film an example of nonverbal communication. Their videos might record something as simple as a short hug, or someone looking at their watch, or even an infant's cries. Then, instead of boring each other with the same "I agree, thank you for sharing that story" comments, the class can dissect each episode and identify the communication that they are witnessing. Authentic discussion, replicated in an online format. UDL to the rescue!

How I Got Here

Ellen Swider

What I enjoyed most about being a student was finding opportunities to own my learning. While I was interested in learning what my instructors taught, I was eager to engage the material in ways that I felt were important and relevant to my own goals. I felt more confident about material that I could relate to and that I could connect to other experiences, and I appreciated the opportunity to experiment with new ideas and make them my own. Students who struggle to engage on a personal level with the curriculum often find it difficult to succeed in college. Therefore, it becomes increasingly important for professors to help students connect their learning to their personal goals. Unfortunately, it is often difficult to facilitate this experience in the college classroom, particularly in the short duration of a semester-long class. By incorporating UDL Guidelines into my planning, however, I have been able to improve my course and better engage and support my students.

I am fortunate to have had both formal preparation in teaching and, throughout my career, the opportunity to teach in various capacities and content areas. My first job out of college was teaching middle school social studies, and I quickly fell in love with it. Years passed, and I taught in several different schools and districts, but I always remained in middle schools. As I became more accomplished with my craft, I began to fully embrace how flexible social studies can be. Social studies is often unfairly characterized as the regurgitation of old dates and events, particularly as they apply to dead White guys. But I found that I had innumerable opportunities to synthesize themes and events with virtually any other topic. In my classes, my students participated in decision-making simulations, conducted independent research projects, and regularly analyzed primary sources to develop their own interpretation of history.

Unfortunately, even though I loved what I was doing, I was becoming increasingly burned out. I wanted to continue offering my students unique learning opportunities, but I could not keep up with the demanding schedule and expectations. A position teaching at the collegiate level presented itself, and I jumped at it. I saw the opportunity to teach in higher education as a chance to focus my efforts on fewer content areas while also injecting some much-needed fun and creativity into higher education.

I have taught and coordinated the communications curriculum at Goodwin University for two years. In this position, I have enthusiastically embraced that same opportunity to be creative and student centered. My students are older and much more disciplined now, but they still thrive on opportunities to engage with curriculum and learning on a personal level, especially as it applies to their career goals.

Ellen received her bachelor of science and master's in education at the University of Connecticut. She is currently working toward a doctoral degree in higher education leadership at the University of Hartford. Her dissertation, titled Latching on to Success: An Exploratory Study of Lactation Support Available to Student-Parents, *explores the lived experiences of breastfeeding student-parents and aims to expose and validate students' experiences and highlight the need for more lactation support on college campuses, particularly for student-parents. Ellen firmly believes that curriculum is never fully written but must be constantly revised and refreshed. Her next UDL challenge is to continue to implement more creative and student-centered UDL activities into the courses she teaches.*

Chapter 6
Nicole Brewer

Practicing Social Justice and Becoming Agents of Change

I am program director of Goodwin University's Professional Studies program, a career-based degree completion program designed to help students develop the skills to advance in their current careers or to explore new opportunities. The degree program culminates in a capstone course, which I have the pleasure of teaching. Students also work with Goodwin's Career Services Team on practical career-based skills, such as creating a résumé, writing a cover letter, and building a professional online presence. This course material and the related assignments give students a chance to prepare themselves for career advancement as soon as they graduate.

While students have found the reflections and the career services aspects of the course satisfying and meaningful, helping students find relevance and value in the course's major project has been more of a challenge.

Before I redesigned the course with UDL in mind, the students were tasked with writing a major research paper on a topic of their choice and then required to give a formal presentation on that topic. The students were required to do in-depth scholarly research on a topic in their field. They were asked to identify a problem in their field and propose or outline possible solutions.

One of the most exciting aspects of teaching the Professional Studies Capstone is that my students come from various fields and study in various disciplines. Some students study health science, while others study business. Some students are already working in their field, such as dental hygiene, and others hope to make a career change by finishing their bachelor's degree and applying to a master's degree program. Students with such differing interests have much to teach each other and much to teach me as well. The potential of this final project was promising, yet final projects for the course always fell short of what I wanted them to be.

Do not get me wrong. My students were hard and diligent workers. They researched problems, found solutions, organized their thoughts, and wrote clear and focused research papers in APA format. They did what they were assigned and did it well. And while teachers should be satisfied with students following directions and producing quality work, I could not shake the feeling that something was off with this major assignment.

My understanding of this assignment changed one semester when I had "Carly" as a student. Carly was a volunteer firefighter who decided to write about improving the mental health of firefighters. Carly was a well-organized, thoughtful student with excellent writing skills. Writing a research paper was right in her wheelhouse. She excelled. Not only was she able to outline the problem and discuss the different solutions presented by experts in the field, but she also outlined some practical steps that departments could take. It was a joy to read her research paper.

Carly was the only student graduating during this particular semester, so she took the course in an independent study format. This meant that her findings and her formal presentation were not widely seen. She had proposed a practical solution, a two-day workshop on mental health for firefighters, in a field in which she was currently working, and hardly anyone had heard what she had to say! Her work had evolved into something much more than an academic assignment; it had the potential to be life changing for a group of people. The fact that she never had the opportunity to present her research to a group of firefighters was a gross failure of the course. Carly had helped me discover exactly what was off about the assignment: it was just an assignment (a means to an end) and should be and could be so much more.

My efforts to revise this assignment started with determining the true goal of the assignment. With formal writing assignments like research papers, the goal of the assignment can get lost. Instructors, myself included, can get bogged down in the technical details of the assignment, such as correctly using APA format, writing grammatically correct sentences, or reaching the page requirements. While formatting, grammar, and page requirements are important, they are not the goal of the assignment. Quite clearly, I needed to clarify the goal of the assignment for both me and my students.

In order to uncover the true goal of the assignment, it was time for me to go back to the heart of it all: social justice. I subscribe to Lee Anne Bell's (2007) definition and understanding of social justice and social justice education. Social justice education calls for creating an environment in which students learn about the unequal social systems that affect people's lives. Social justice education can help students understand the way in which oppression and inequality work in society. Additionally, social justice education should go one step further by giving students the skills and tools to analyze and evaluate what they learned, to develop ways to disrupt these unequal social systems, and to create conditions for social change in their own communities. More simply, one of the goals of social justice education is to guide students to become agents of change. The major assignment for the Professional Studies Capstone has the potential to include this fundamental purpose of social justice education. The lens of social justice education allowed me to shift the goal of the capstone project.

The original focus of the assignment, unintentionally so, had become the task of writing a research paper. Sure, students could choose the topics that were most interesting and relevant to them, but writing a quality paper had become the goal. Social justice education is bigger, more influential, and more impactful than completing a research paper. Therefore, the goal of the assignment needed to reflect this reality. The goal of the assignment is now for students to *propose a solution to a problem in their field and develop a way to present that solution to stakeholders.*

With the goal clearer in my mind, I next tackled the barriers that prevented students from achieving that goal. What were the barriers? And how would I eliminate them? I thought back to Carly and how the assignment fell short for her. The assignment did not allow her to share her knowledge with her community. The assignment held her back from becoming an agent of change, someone who could make a real difference in her professional and personal world.

The most conspicuous obstacle this assignment presented for students was the requirement of a formal presentation. Was a formal presentation really necessary to achieve the new assignment goal? Quite clearly, the answer was no. In fact, this formal presentation requirement was limiting students' ability to achieve the assignment goal. First of all, formal presentations might not be relevant to a student's professional field. A dental hygienist who wants to create a system in which parents are better informed about dental X-rays for their children may find that another presentation mode, such as a poster or infographic, is more effective at communicating a message to stakeholders than a formal presentation. A preschool teacher who is promoting the benefits of including an appreciation of nature in a school's curriculum might choose to conduct a short sample lesson for a group of interested teachers instead of standing in front of a group with an electronic slide presentation.

Other limitations of formal presentations have more to do with students' comfort level and the general environment of the class. For example, many students are terrified of formal, public presentations. While public speaking can be an important skill, it is not a requirement of the class, and it seemed completely unnecessary for students to practice this skill yet again after taking a required communications course as part of the degree program, especially when public speaking is not necessary to achieve the goal of the project. In addition, while giving a formal presentation is a simple way for other students in the class to learn about the work their classmates completed, technology provides a multitude of ways for students to share their work with their peers. Creative use of discussion boards on learning management systems gives students opportunities to review their peers' work and to respond with encouragement and constructive feedback.

My first consideration in my revision efforts for this assignment was the principle of Engagement. To guide the changes I made to the assignment, I focused on employing strategies for recruiting interest by optimizing individual choice and autonomy and by enhancing relevance, value, and authenticity. The assignment had always given students a choice for their topic, but my revision has helped make the assignment much more relevant to the students' interests and lives. When students are given more control over the design of their presentations, the assignment becomes much more meaningful because it relates to their professional field and requires them to think more deeply about the stakeholders in their professional field. They begin to ask questions like, *Who needs to hear this information the most? Who has a stake in the problem? Who can help me make a difference? What is the best way to reach my audience?* Students can also continue to hone the skills they need in their professional field by learning and developing ways to communicate information in a format that is most relevant to their field.

I next considered the principle of Action and Expression as I worked to revise the capstone project. I was specifically inspired by the UDL emphasis on using multiple media for communication as I made additional changes to the assignment. I encourage students to be creative with their presentations. Oral presentations with slide shows are not required! Posters, podcasts, commercials, and flyers are just some of the ways students can present their research. There are no restrictions for presentation mode. Instead, I ask students to justify the type of presentation they decide to use by asking themselves questions about their audience or stakeholders: *How can I best explain the problem I researched to a group of volunteer firefighters? How can I show a group of educators the benefits of this new curriculum I researched? How would a group of small business owners respond to a 15-minute podcast on my research? What is the best way to reach a group of veterans to explain the importance of my research?*

Once I applied UDL to this research project, I had a scaffolded assignment that encouraged students to see themselves as agents of change in a field that is meaningful to them:

In addition to completing the 10–15-page research paper, you are also required to present your argument to a wider audience. The format of the presentation is your choice. However, the presentation mode must be appropriate for the field, profession, or topic of your research project. Some examples of possible presentation modes include a formal in-person oral presentation, an infographic, a recorded narrated PowerPoint presentation uploaded to YouTube, a short podcast episode, a print advertisement, a press release, or a commercial. You will be required to meet with your instructor to help you generate ideas, to get feedback, and to complete a research project presentation proposal before submitting the project presentation.

Asking students to think about presenting their research to those in their field has allowed students to make important connections between their schoolwork and their professional lives. Giving students the guidance to make these types of connections is critical in a Professional Studies degree program. However, while students claim to feel connected to their projects and presentations in a way that was not apparent before the revision work, I believe there is more I can do to improve this project. The presentation is still a bit of an afterthought in relation to the research paper. Students spend much of their time and energy working on the research paper and do not put as much thought and effort into the presentation. If I am honest about the structure of the course, the students are not truly given the time and space to be creative with the presentation process. I have more reflection to do about this project, but I believe the best way to overcome this particular barrier is to shift the focus of the project from the paper to the presentation. With this shift, I must ask a new question: *Is a formal research paper really necessary in order to complete the desired course goal?* Addressing this question opens up even more possibilities for Professional Studies students.

As I think about the next steps in making more improvements to the course, I push myself to keep in mind the transformative nature of education and, of course, UDL. While writing and researching well, developing effective leadership skills, and creating a polished résumé are all essential and vital professional skills, I cannot lose sight of the importance of helping students envision their ultimate potential as professionals and members of a community. When barriers are removed, students become the focus, and the classroom becomes a nurturing space full of growth, expansion, and immeasurable possibility.

How I Got Here

Nicole Brewer

I never saw myself as a teacher, especially since I did not like school as a young person. The classroom was not a comfortable place for me. I was a shy, quiet Black girl who lived and went to school in an almost exclusively White community. I had a hard time connecting with the other students, and sometimes students and even teachers rejected me because of my difference. School was painful and lonely, so when I graduated from high school, I felt freed.

My undergraduate and graduate experience was better than my high school experience. I had many moments of feeling nurtured, challenged, and accepted by professors and other students. I began to understand how transformative the classroom could be. I started to learn how the classroom could become a place in which students can shape and reshape themselves into greater, more expansive versions of themselves. When I was a young person, the classroom made me feel small and insignificant. In college, the classroom was the place where I learned I could do and be more than I ever thought possible.

After a few years of career exploration, I eventually found myself in a community college classroom teaching English composition. It was not where I expected to be, and at the time, I was not sure it was where I wanted to be; however, I accepted the part-time teaching position. When I started teaching, I was disappointed with where I had ended up professionally. As a graduate student, I wanted to do social justice work. I wanted to work with a nonprofit organization "righting the wrongs of society." I wanted to combat bigotry and inequality head on. It took me time to appreciate that social justice work can be done in the college classroom.

As a student I had two drastically different classroom experiences, and I carry those divergent experiences with me as a teacher. As a beginning teacher, I used those experiences to shape my teaching style, and over 10 years later as an assistant professor of English and humanities, I continue to use these contrasting class-room experiences to motivate me. The environments of these two classrooms remind me of the incredible power of education: it can constrain, or it can liberate.

Education is an important tool in social justice work. I teach because I believe in equity. I believe that every person should know that what they say, do, and feel matters. Education and knowledge have the ability to create a human existence in which every individ-ual truly knows they have the power and significance to impact the world.

I was drawn to Universal Design for Learning because UDL is a natural extension of the social justice work I have always wanted to do. UDL describes the learning environment much in the same way that I see the cultural, social, economic, and political environment when I think about social justice work. UDL asks educators to find ways to eliminate the barriers in the learning environment that limit students' success. Social justice work can do the same thing for soci-ety that UDL can do for the classroom by finding ways to eliminate the barriers that racism, sexism, ableism, homophobia, and other forms of bigotry create for certain groups in society.

Nicole received her master's degree from New York University, and she is currently pursuing a doctoral degree in education from Northeastern Uni-versity. She coauthored a book with her father titled Withstanding the Lie, *which helps people cope with the mental and emotional harm caused by bigotry. Nicole's next UDL challenge is to explore the ways in which UDL can enhance institution-wide academic supports to improve student retention and persistence in higher education.*

Chapter 7

Zachary Vincent Smith

From Standard Operating Procedures to Universal Design for Learning: A Lifelong Learning Process

History courses at the undergraduate level are normally heavily lecture based. Having sat through many of these courses, I wanted to figure out how to engage all my students on multiple levels. When I had the opportunity to teach my own Introduction to World History course, I began reconsidering my use of lectures and PowerPoints. I was using slides and words to engage my class, but I found myself wondering if my lectures and PowerPoints were accessible to all types of learners. I asked myself, "Why has PowerPoint been one of my main modes for transferring information to students?" This is where I decided to create interactive class sessions using the principles of UDL.

I decided to incorporate a UDL-informed approach into my unit on the Great Depression, European dictators, and the American New Deal. When creating a PowerPoint, one typically starts with a title page displaying the topic of the lecture. For some students, the words alone will grab their attention. But what about other types of learners? I decided to revise the lesson in a way that reflected the UDL emphasis on using multiple media for communication to enhance the experience for all students.

The beginning of any course is the ideal time to grab students' attention and get them excited about the topic, so rather than merely presenting an opening slide that led into the lecture and unit activities, I added marching sounds to the PowerPoint slide. While the words are shown on the screen, the audio starts softly and grows louder as the students file into the classroom. After about two minutes, I yell "March!" and just like that, the students invariably begin marching in place. Then, I yell "Get in sync!" and the students start counting and performing a uniform march. I can hear them saying "One, two. One, two" as they work together to be in sync while marching in place. I then proceed to ask students who are not able to keep up with the rest of their classmates to sit down. One student asked why, and I explained that there is no room for an individual in a fascist society. I explain that a student sitting down represents the eradication of an individual in this type of society. After the students have marched for two minutes, I yell "Stop!" I then ask the students why they started to march. The most common response is "You told us to." When I ask them "Why would you listen to me?" they reply, "Because you are the professor." I then grab a bundle of pencils. I explain to the students the definition of fascism and how they, a group of pencils together, cannot be broken. I remove one pencil from the bundle and break it. I say to the students, "That is what happens when you step out of the standard operating procedures."

This interactive exercise is a great way to lead into a conversation about how people fall in line under fascist dictators. The "multiple means" encompassed by the music, the title slide, the students' own behavior, and their interactions with their classmates all operate together to demonstrate a fundamental lesson about the dynamics of social conformity. This activity also helps the students actively move in the classroom to get their brains prepared for the work that is about to come. Students have presented multiple perspectives regarding this marching exercise. Some students could not believe that this is how basic society can be. Other students conclude that many people just follow the standard operating procedures and never notice what is really going on around them.

UDL reminds us that it is important to build in periodic reminders of both the goal and its value for students as a way of motivating them to sustain effort and concentration in the face of distractions. I include a slide dedicated to the objectives of the class that tells the students exactly what they are supposed to learn from this unit.

Having these questions posted gives the students a sense of how to direct their attention while participating in this unit. It also gives me an opportunity to ask students what they already know about these topics before we even begin. Exploring these objectives before beginning the unit activities gives students an opportunity to discover as a class what background knowledge they have about the subject matter and helps them understand how the topic can relate to the current world. Students are normally eager to share experiences from their own lives and to talk about how these issues continue to directly affect them in today's world. Many students point out how the promise of "simple solutions for complex issues" continues to be a calling card for extreme groups on both sides of the spectrum. Other students take a more microscale look at how the Treaty of Versailles is directly to blame for contemporary problems regarding territorial and political sovereignty for nations all over the world.

In what I like to call the "body paragraphs" of my unit, I use multiple ways for students to interact with me and the material. In consideration of the value UDL pedagogy places on employing multiple media for communication, I present different kinds of learning materials to enhance the students' experience. For example, I use a primary source letter written by a German soldier to his family and the response from his sister. I then ask the students to talk about the difference in tone and ideologies between the soldier and his sister. Students have the option to respond to the prompt using a Jamboard that has been built into the lecture slide or to openly discuss the prompt in the classroom with the class. Using primary source documents gives students a different perspective from the current standard in many schools of learning only about the leaders and big names of history. Primary source analysis is key for history students who want to know what really was going on in society and who want to learn more than just what the big names had to say. Primary sources also provide a great tool for explaining to students that their everyday writing could be a primary source document used later in history. Allowing the use of the Jamboard gives students who are not comfortable with public speaking the opportunity to privately post their thoughts and feelings about the source and still participate in class. Students enjoy the Australian ballot style of posting because they can express themselves freely without putting a claim to that thought process. Using multiple means of action and expression also supports students who have text- or language-related disabilities. Students can engage with the material by drawing a picture on the Jamboard or posting a meme or music clip to show that they understood the question and are able to process it in a way that is meaningful to them. Students have produced pictures depicting dehumanization tactics that the soldier's family would have experienced back in Germany. Many students feel as if the soldier's words go unheeded because of the way German society operated during World War I. The soldier is expressing his true feelings about being on a battlefield, and his feelings are completely negated by his sister's response. Students are very aware that indoctrination in societies is common and extremely dangerous. Students then take it upon themselves to figure out how and why we still use dehumanization tactics in today's world.

I also created a dueling speech activity as a part of this unit. In this activity, the students watch two speeches, one by Oswald Mosley and the other by Charlie Chaplin. During the first viewing, the two speech clips are playing at the same time. The students have a minute to write down what they think the speeches are about. After that minute, the students watch both clips one at a time and take a minute to discuss what the speeches are saying. Again, using multiple media for communication, students can access the information and work with it. Rather than just watching a video clip and moving on, students are pushed to engage in academic discourse about the content. The video clips allow students to engage with the material in other ways, and they can make further critical assessments of the ideas presented by the speakers. This activity enhances the students' understanding of how everyday people fail to think for themselves. Students start to make connections with the present day as they come to understand that leaders, even in our current time, use rhetorical tactics to attract populations to dehumanizing ideologies.

At the conclusion of the unit, the students reevaluate the essential questions by participating in a short, open-forum discussion about how their ideas about fascism have changed or developed because of their participation in the interactive lesson. By allowing for this reexamination of their thought process, I can immediately see how the students have responded to the unit. Students can answer the essential questions posed at the beginning of the class in whatever medium they choose. They can draw a picture or a chart, write a paragraph, have a conversation with a classmate, or post a video or audio file to the class learning management system (LMS). This diversity of action and expression allows students to communicate their own thoughts in their own way while still participating in a common learning experience.

As higher education continues to change and evolve, one thing that will stay the same is the need for students to actively engage in their learning. By adopting Universal Design for Learning, I have made a difference in students' lives by making my classroom more accessible to all learners. Knowing that UDL is about constantly improving our work as educators, I continue to be a student of UDL as I strive to further develop my skills in the classroom. Through UDL, I discovered new ways to express my personal approach to teaching, and I have developed a language that helps me to explain my reasons for teaching the way that I do.

How I Got Here

Zachary Vincent Smith

How does one get to Universal Design for Learning after years of experience with what I like to call the standard operating procedures (SOPs) of education? SOPs refer to the way things have always been done, a set of instructions handed down year after year. SOPs work, or seem to, because they provide a codified set of rules that everyone knows. It is also the case, however, that the unquestioned reliance on SOPs causes people, classrooms, and societies to repeat mistake after mistake under the name of rule and tradition. For me, moving away from standard operating procedures has been a lifelong journey of personal learning and educational experimentation.

Growing up in the small farming community of Elkhorn, Wisconsin, I never imagined I would become a teacher. Looking back at my early school years, I now know I was a different kind of learner: just as bright but simply different. Sitting in class was a struggle, and I was labeled an "excessive socializer." The SOPs of the education system did not work for me. I personally experienced the degree to which the standard type of teacher-centered instruction can reify class, race, and social structures and can block learning and advancement in the name of arbitrary benchmarks.

Early in my life, I planned on becoming a professional rugby player, but after a traumatic brain injury, I had to examine what I was going to do with my life. My favorite subject is history, so I took some history courses at a local community college. After taking Introduction to World History and European History, I fell in love with using historical narrative to learn how the world worked. I then moved on to earn my bachelor's degree in history. While earning my bachelor's degree, I discovered that I wanted to be a history teacher.

Unfortunately, when I graduated with my bachelor's degree in history, the teaching market was not looking good, so I fell back into the family business and obeyed family SOPs by following in my father's and older brother's footsteps. I enrolled at a police academy and took the training to become a police officer, and for a few years, I worked in law enforcement. However, this life clearly was not for me, so this time, going against SOP, I decided to pursue a master's degree in Holocaust and genocide studies. My mentor helped me explore how I could become a better historian. My unusual background led me to want to learn about the worst things on the planet and ways to fix them. More specifically, I wanted to learn how people could become complicit in oppressive systems of state-sponsored violence. I wanted to learn how deference to authority, following SOPs, could go extremely wrong.

After I graduated with my master's in Holocaust and genocide studies, I found a job at a private high school in Connecticut. My teaching methods, which involved jumping up and down, changing the pitch of my voice, playing games (such as "Trench-Pong"[1]), and creating new interactive assignments, were met with utter disparagement by the administration. Even though the students were laughing, learning, and having intellectual discussions, my teaching methods were challenged. I again found myself questioning standard operating procedures. This time, however, I was questioning them in the field of education.

My studies into the history of genocide impressed me with the profound damage that can result from the blind acceptance of tradition and societal devotion to the SOP of history. I carried this

---

[1] Trench-Pong is a game I created to introduce the students to interconnected realms of killing space during World War I. This game involves groups of students building trenches and lofting tennis balls from a distance to figure out the death toll caused by artillery.

awareness into the classroom, where it caused me to think skeptically about traditional pedagogical practices.

A few years later, I began teaching history at Goodwin University, where I was introduced to UDL. Little did I know that my unique experiences as a rugby player, a historian, a police officer, and a high school teacher could be brought together through UDL, which can be understood as a kind of tool for prying apart the assumptions of educational SOP. I also found that UDL provided me with the support and the means to embrace and enhance my unusual teaching style and to reassess my own classroom practice.

Zachary received his master of arts in Holocaust and genocide studies from West Chester University of Pennsylvania. His recent publication, "The Guatemalan Genocide of Film: An Ongoing Crisis and Omission," can be found in the book The History of Genocide in Cinema: Atrocities on Screen. *Zachary's next UDL challenge is to continue to advance UDL strategies by redesigning history curriculum and incorporating UDL into asynchronous learning by creating more interactive assignments for accessibility.*

Composition

Chapter 8

Dana C. Sheehan

Breaking Down the Introduction Paragraph With UDL Trickery

n every Introductory Composition course, there comes a point when the students have to put together a formal research essay. The students must make their readers pay attention to what they are saying and possibly persuade them to believe a certain side. I've seen students have issues with many different aspects of this assignment, but one crucial part that many students struggle with is the very first step: getting started. The challenge of introducing an idea in a way that makes it interesting, engaging, and accessible holds many student writers back, just as it also hinders would-be writers everywhere. A lesson I put through some major UDL reconstruction was one on introduction paragraphs.

Writing an introduction paragraph is nerve wracking for many people. Think of it as the opening to a first date or the first 15 seconds of a telemarketer's call. For some, this skill comes quite easily, but for most, it is the last thing they ever want to do. Students typically fumble around for a few sentences, trying to say something but not really making sense. They toss in a final sentence they hope covers the main point of their idea, that dreaded thesis statement, and then they move on to the rest of the essay, forgetting everything that they just did. Does this sound familiar to anyone? After seeing this class after class for many years, I realized that there had to be a relatively painless way to show students different ways to write an introduction paragraph. Challenge given and challenge accepted.

Taking on the goal of figuring out a way to lecture less and engage the classroom more, I turned to my first love, television. I picked a few television shows, some movie openings, and even podcast introductions to show students different ways, visual and auditory, that ideas can be introduced to an audience. My first go-to tends to be visual, since I find that visual media is more easily understood in this day and age of quick video clips and flashy action movies. Many students also find it easy to translate these visual examples into writing.

I made sure to select introductions from a variety of different genres so that students could see the many different options for introducing their topics. As an example, National Geographic tends to open their specials with beautiful pictures. True crime television shows open by taking us into the scene of a crime. A TED Talk begins with a specific chime and an amazing storyteller on a red, round carpet. I also encourage my students to consider the opening hooks used to introduce podcasts and radio news programs. All of these begin differently, all of them are perfect for their particular contexts, and they are all distinct and brilliant in their own ways.

I start my lesson on introductions by showing one clip of a television show and asking the class to break it down. While we have this conversation, I slide key terms into the discussion to help the students feel comfortable using academic terms to explain the clip. (This will help when I transition to the topic of writing their essays.) I continue to do the same thing for two or three more clips from television shows or movies. Once I feel the students have gotten the hang of this, I move on to a few different podcasts and continue using the key terms, encouraging the students to bring the terminology up before I do.

Breaking down visual and auditory introductions worked really well for some students, but it did not work for everyone. I found that there were still students who couldn't make the connection from television or podcast/radio to their own writing. I was able to explain introductory strategies, but some students struggled to put them into practice. So I started to include examples of introduction paragraphs after the podcasts. I would have the students break the sample introductions down by sentence and discuss the terms we were using with the videos and the podcasts. I had the best results when I would do this section of the class in groups, having each group work on a different example of an introduction paragraph. Having examples in writing was helpful for some of the students who were confused by the multimedia examples, but I found that students who hated writing and had relatively little belief in their own skill were still struggling to write effective introductory paragraphs. This is where the final activity came in.

Students work best when they are allowed to stretch their brains. If professors can figure out a way to help them do that in the classroom, then when the students get outside of the classroom they will be able to work with the information they have retained. I started to incorporate different kinds of group activities, from creating their own television introduction to giving them a random topic to create an essay about and having them figure out how they would open that essay. I've also made it part of the lesson to give them time to flesh out ideas about their own essays. I do, however, give the stipulation that they can't come up with just one idea for their essay; they have to come up with three. That way they can stretch their own imagination and see different ways to accomplish their goals. I love using the phrase "There's always another way" with my classes, and composition classes especially, so students don't feel stuck when one way doesn't work for them.

One of the challenges that I have seen students face in their introductory composition course is that they haven't had the experience writing essays that are academic, are in the third person, are research based, or aren't just stories about themselves. A lot of time in class is spent trying to retrain students to write less like they are writing a text message and more like they are writing a formal academic assignment. (I love challenging students to start writing in complete sentences while texting and to break away from emojis—it's incredibly fun to hear the stories that come from that.) I have also found in my experience working with different kinds of students that, regardless of where I have taught, students are always coming from various educational backgrounds and with many emotional blocks toward writing, and it will always take time to break down these barriers and get students on the same page. Thankfully, Universal Design for Learning taught me first and foremost to identify the main goal as a way of solving any problem I am having. The main goal of this introduction paragraph lesson was to help as many students as possible find the varying options for their introduction paragraph. So many times, students will feel overwhelmed and out of control. If I can show them how to control the scaffolding behind every aspect of their assignment, such as in this lesson about their introduction paragraphs, they will have no problem letting their ideas shine through. I just have to show them some options.

When I was in school, there was a short set of rules that went along with the various kinds of essays students wrote throughout their academic tenure. Those rules still exist, but I needed to make sure that all of the students felt they had the ability to make their essays their own with as many options as possible. Without exposure to examples of different kinds of introductions, including multimedia examples (the videos and podcasts), the idea of sitting down and starting an essay could (and does) sound daunting to people who aren't as in love with the English language as I am. In the initial planning of this introduction paragraph class, I knew my goal first and identified what I wanted the students to learn and walk away with. My next step was to show them how to have fun with their introduction paragraphs and how to make them their own. And then I needed to let them do it in a place where they could ask questions and thrive.

I've been teaching and recalculating this lesson on introduction paragraphs for three years now. When it started, we only discussed the visual introductions. The lesson has evolved over each class and each semester, and it now includes podcasts, sample written introductions, and various activities to help students understand how to apply a variety of introductory strategies to their own assignments. I have found that the rate of creative introduction paragraphs has increased substantially after this class because I've shown students so many different ways to understand introductions, as well as just how important they are (and how much fun they can be).

Keeping all of what I just wrote in mind, I have to say that with every course in which I include multiple ways of learning, there are always students who prefer the more text-based way of teaching, and those students tend to feel like there isn't a need for the visual or auditory examples. For the most part, though, those students are getting more and more rare. By incorporating visual, auditory, and written examples of introductory strategies, I have been able to achieve a higher rate of understanding. And the students, by and large, love the idea of watching something that has nothing to do with English composition, only to realize at the end of the class that they accidentally (on their part) learned how to write introduction paragraphs.

How I Got Here

Dana Sheehan

When I was growing up, my grandmother always told me that I would make an excellent teacher. My grandmother and grandfather watched me create storylines on their ancient chalkboard in front of the fire while they would watch the evening news. My grandmother watched me stay up past my bedtime filling my notebooks with stories and being more excited about what I was creating than any game she could have put in front of me. I have always had a love of writing and a love of story. I have also always had a love of the rules of English and how to challenge them creatively. As I got older, though, my chalkboard turned into a television, my love of story evolved into a love of movies, my grandmother's voice faded, and I decided to take my love of story and become a screenwriter in the glittery land of Hollywood. I spent many years working in the television industry, and my love of writing slowly became hidden behind the long work schedule and the confinements of network television. I was trying to follow rules that I didn't necessarily enjoy, and I wasn't having the creative fun that I used to have when all I needed was a journal, my mind, and some time. My job became just a paycheck, which I had sworn I would never let happen. I eventually left La-La Land and went back to school for my MFA in creative writing in the hopes I would get my creative spark back. I was going to write my first novel. It wasn't my initial goal to go back to school to become a teacher, but one of the perks of going back to school was the option to have my degree paid for if I became a teaching assistant. The responsible adult in me was very excited at the idea of writing my first novel in a college environment for free. With my grandmother's voice in the forefront of my mind telling me how great a teacher I would be, I signed on. Little did I know that checking the box to become a TA would send my life on a very different path and that I would love every moment of it.

As a teaching assistant, I was lucky enough to teach two courses every semester. I had two courses each semester to try out new-to-me ideas and to find my legs as a professor. I remember the first time I was discussing the need for thesis statements and for a type of order within an essay. I was new and I didn't have all of the answers, but I had what worked for me. I have a distinct memory of a day when I stood back from the chalkboard I had been scribbling notes all over and asked the class if they understood what I was saying. Four students made eye contact with me and nodded. That sounds small, and it is, but it was the first time *four students* actually acknowledged that I had taught them something they didn't understand before. It was as if their nods were a drug. I was hooked.

This passion to help students learn grew from watching them simply understand my words to having them start critically processing ideas in order to formulate their own opinions and eventually to reframe their learning process in a way that worked for them. I started to see students create their own ideas and bring what they'd learned in the classroom into their own lives outside of school. When Universal Design for Learning (UDL) found me, I was ready for my next step in learning. I needed guidance on how to help more students at the same time. I knew how to help people who learned the way I learned, but that was not enough. I had to help more. UDL opened that door, and my classrooms, in person and online, changed as a result.

I've always considered myself a nerd for learning. Enabling students to learn by using their strengths, and figuring out how to help them work with their weaknesses are necessary skills for any teacher. As I've started learning about and implementing UDL into my classrooms and into my way of life, I've become much more focused on finding interesting ways to teach so every student can learn.

I've been an English professor for the better part of a decade now, and the level of excitement that I feel with every new semester is exponentially higher than what I felt when I was living in Los Angeles and working around scripts and television sets. The creativity I am able to see each week in my students, regardless of the course, gives me more inspiration than I had when I was given free rein as a student in my creative writing courses in college. The pedagogy of UDL has shown me that what matters is not how I like to teach but how students like to learn. My mind is constantly churning for ways to help more students understand my goals for their course. I am constantly coming up with new ideas to make sure that all different kinds of learners learn, and it is a lot of work. I cannot deny that. I spend many extra hours looking for additional ways to help all students understand what they need to know. Creating a game is much more involved than lecturing at a board, talking to students who have stopped listening. The attentiveness that I have in my classroom (even my 8 am classes) has more than doubled. I never expected UDL would do that, and I would never be able to go backward from here. I have only just cracked the door to using UDL in my classrooms, both online and in person. This pedagogy allows my nerd-for-learning mentality to always be excited about the next idea or the new group of students. One of my favorite side effects of UDL is that my courses never go stale. Knowing that no two students are ever the same and no cohort of students is the same means that things will have to change every semester. It makes each class more alive for me and for the students. I will be a professor for the rest of my life. There is no profession that suits me better, makes me feel more alive, and has allowed me so much creativity. When I think back to my childhood and my grandmother who told me that I should be a teacher, I now admit wholeheartedly, 30-some-odd years later, that my grandmother was indeed right.

Dana received her BFA in writing, literature, and publishing from Emerson College and her MFA in creative and professional writing from Western Connecticut State University. She has delivered UDL-infused presentations at conferences all around New England—her latest in-person one was called "Transforming Practice Into a Game: A Plus 1 for Fun," about the importance of having games in the classroom. Dana's next UDL challenge will be about making discussion boards more inviting.

Chapter 9

Cynthia J. Murphy

Minimizing Threats and Distractions in a Peer Review

One incident that took place in a developmental English class stands out as a critical moment in my teaching practice. It came time in the class for students to exchange paper drafts in small, assigned groups, to read and evaluate each other's writing and to provide feedback with the goal of helping each other improve their drafts. One student, R, did not move from her seat to join her small group. The other two members of her group began working without her, while R sat alone at her desk writing in her notebook. I approached R, knelt to her eye level, and quietly reminded her of what the class was doing. She told me that she could not work in small groups; she preferred to work alone: "I can't work like that." She appeared anxious, shifting her focus from me quickly back to her notebook. I felt compelled to let her be so that she could feel most comfortable and get her work done the way she knew best, so I did just that, understanding that independent work is one of many multiple paths to learning. We were friendly, talking for a little while about her project, and then I just left her to write independently for the rest of the 20-minute class activity. It was relatively unremarkable for a critical moment. This student was otherwise very respectful and generally participated in class discussions. I could have just moved on. But the incident nagged at me. It reminded me of the many times I would walk around the room during peer review to see if anyone needed my help, often to find that students were off task, or had finished at rocket speed, or were otherwise disengaged. Or, like R, respectfully declining participation. As an observer of these kinds of exchanges for many years over the course of my career, I had a strong sense that some students had a negative perception of peer review. Sure, there were always those who invited peer review, but the majority seemed to participate perfunctorily. Still, I continue to assign peer review, always striving to make it a better experience. I know how peer review improves student writing, mimics professional practice, and allows students to build soft skills, those interpersonal competencies that are so important in school and in the workforce. Moreover, social construction and collaborative interaction are integral to the tenets of the writing process; therefore, I felt tasked with supporting my students to make peer review as nonthreatening and as meaningful as possible. To engage and prepare all my students, I knew I had to make more changes to how I assigned and implemented peer review so students could reap these benefits.

One of the most important principles of Universal Design for Learning is its emphasis on identifying and eliminating barriers to learning. One barrier that I addressed with UDL pedagogy was the presence of potential threats to the positive social and emotional environment of the classroom during peer review. The solution was to build interpersonal communication and to enhance levels of trust and safety in the classroom. The first goal of revamping my pedagogical approach, therefore, was to provide examples of how to give and receive feedback to help students practice effective peer review strategies and to gradually increase their degree of peer review literacy. To build these fluencies, I needed to offer multitiered levels of support, and I began to implement this support in three phases. In the first phase, I tap into students' prior knowledge to construct a class definition of peer review. This sets the stage for building upon students' prior knowledge and lays the groundwork for further instruction. In this initial phase, we discuss the benefits of peer review as well as any negative perceptions of the practice. The open class discussion, along with the class-constructed peer review definition on the board, works well to create collective interest and investment in the topic. This conversation also helps to dismantle any negative perceptions or dread that students may harbor regarding peer review, and it helps to build confidence and a shared understanding. In the second phase, I provide models of a successful peer review. I break down the practice into a formula they can use for verbalizing their critique to their peers, but they start by practicing this formula on an anonymous sample student paper. Practicing responses on samples helps give students the tools they need to communicate their critiques safely. In addition, modeling and providing simulations of effective peer feedback helps students to develop a better understanding of what peer review looks like in action. In the third phase, I assign students to small groups of two or three, assigning specific roles to group members and providing explicit instructions on what they need to do and the time allotment for the activity. These strategies help foster more successful peer interactions, optimizing the effectiveness and impact of the peer review process.

This scaffolded, incremental approach to introducing peer review reduces social and emotional barriers to students' participation in this collaborative learning activity. As part of this peer review literacy training, students respond to a sample paper. Instead of having them start cold, with no training or instruction, the sample peer review activity gives students practice so they know how to participate thoughtfully and effectively. I first provide a minilesson on three levels of feedback: destructive, constructive, and instructive. I explain that destructive feedback is feedback that does not help anyone. It offers a blanket negative critique with no example or explanation. Examples of destructive feedback include statements like "This is all over the place" or "This is not very clear." Comments like these do nothing to explain what is wrong with the paper. Moreover, they may have a damaging effect on the interpersonal peer relationship or jeopardize the collaborative spirit of the classroom. I have students think of some other examples of destructive feedback. The responses often elicit vibrant discussions. For some unknown reason, they often have fun giving destructive feedback to an imaginary peer. Next, I explain that constructive feedback is feedback that starts with a praise comment, then follows it by pointing out an area in need of attention. An example of constructive feedback might be something like "This topic is relevant. The thesis sentence, however, is not clear in your introduction" or "Great job with APA formatting. The paper gets off track in the second paragraph." Using the sample paper as a guide, students practice providing constructive feedback. The last type of feedback that I teach them about is instructive feedback. This, I explain, is the type of feedback that they want to provide to one another. This is the best type of feedback because, first, it provides a praise comment, which can be helpful to set a positive tone. This is then followed by the student pointing out an area that needs improvement and indicating a specific line or segment of the paper to illustrate that need. Finally, the student offers a suggestion of how to improve it (an example revision). The formula I provide for instructive feedback is praise + detect + suggest (PDS). For example, an instructive comment might go something like this: "You've done a wonderful job convincing me of your point of view on this argument (praise). The second paragraph gets a little off topic. Here is a sentence that veers in a different direction (detect). To revise, I suggest that you delete that line (suggest)." Again, using the sample paper as a guide, my students practice providing instructive feedback using the PDS formula, the model paper, and the imaginary student before they ever provide and receive feedback on each other's work. The practice using an anonymous sample, therefore, minimizes threat and increases student peer review literacy, all while building students' sense of trust and psychological safety.

These small changes in peer review instruction and practice have helped students like R increase levels of trust in themselves and in their competency to provide valuable feedback. They also gain an understanding of the role of peer review not only in writing, but across disciplines and into the workplace. I found that having a class conversation about a sample paper takes the focus off their own writing and shifts it onto the writing process itself as a collaborative practice. This lesson minimizes the threat of hurting peers' feelings, and it also allows them a safe space to practice detecting and verbalizing feedback. Another positive effect of these peer review lesson changes is that the class conversation, the practice feedback (especially the destructive feedback), and the support of a formula all combine to build a fun and positive classroom culture where everyone participates.

The UDL principle of identifying student-centered solutions to overcoming barriers to learning is reflected in the teaching styles of my favorite and most memorable professors, it aligns with commonsense thinking, and it is consistent with what we know about how students develop communication literacies. The revision step of the writing process relies on outside perspectives and feedback from a critical audience, which can be uncomfortable for some and which, in some cases, can sabotage opportunities for growth. Students don't want to hurt their peers' feelings, or they are not yet confident in their own ability to offer valuable feedback. Sometimes, too, they simply don't trust the advice of their peers. However, I have learned firsthand how valuable peer review is, both as a writing student gaining literacy in this practice and as a teacher trying to help my students learn to write with greater confidence. As a student learning the craft of storytelling, I found the feedback of my peers in creative writing workshops to be helpful when pinpointing aspects of my writing that needed work or that I had overlooked. I also found that, as I gained experience providing feedback to my peers, my own writing skill improved. When peer review is implemented effectively and instructively, I see the learning process in action. Students help each other as reviewers and reviewees; they make neural and social connections. These are the very conditions necessary for deepest learning. I continue to draw from the UDL pedagogy in the changing landscape of teaching and learning, with face-to-face, virtual, synchronous, asynchronous, online, remote, hybrid, and all the yet-to-be-discovered pathways in education. For meaningful educational experiences, I believe social connections matter. These newly formed social connections can be fragile and require an atmosphere that is safe and free from psychosocial threat. The UDL solutions of minimizing threat, building positive classroom collaboration, providing samples and models of instruction, and supplying guidelines and instructions for small group work are invaluable to the overall organization and success of each class session.

Although the time with my student, R, had passed well before I put these meaningful changes into practice, hopefully telling this story recounts an important lesson. Armed with UDL pedagogy, my confidence has risen. Whenever I am met with that same look of fear and uncertainty that R wore when faced with the prospect of peer review, I will know how to respond. I am confident that with time, patience, and practice, I can provide a classroom landscape that prioritizes social and emotional support and fosters the kind of positive collaboration that is instrumental to peer review and, ultimately, to the improvement of writing skills.

How I Got Here

Cynthia J. Murphy

I've always been drawn to memories and to the pleasure of recounting them with family and friends, new and old. There's something magical about the ability of storytelling to connect human to human, to create bonds, and to reinforce lived experience. This love of story, whether the tale reflects the miraculous, the devastating, or the everyday, is what brought me to the teaching profession over 17 years ago. My undergraduate and graduate degree focus was creative writing, where I could hone the storytelling craft. One of the core practices in the field of creative writing is the inclusion of writing workshops that are heavily centered on peer review. Generally, peer review entails students exchanging drafts of their writing projects and providing and receiving critical feedback, with the goal of collaborating to produce better writing. For more extroverted students, this practice seemingly presents little resistance or suffering. However, in reflecting on my own experience with writing workshops, I recall the sense of fear and overall discomfort when it was my turn in the roundtable to receive or provide peer critiques. Perhaps it was the classroom climate, or perhaps my freshman inexperience, but in my first days and months of exposure to writing workshops, I often felt like I was sitting in the proverbial hot seat, clutching my desk for support and waiting for a shift in focus to someone, anyone, or anything else. As the provider of feedback, I stumbled over my assessment, fearful of impairing fragile peer friendships, and unsure whether I was meeting the criteria of a proficient peer reviewer. Of course, after gaining more familiarity with this practice, I became accustomed to it and worried less and less. It became an expected—and eventually a welcomed—part of the process of writing. I learned to recognize the value of peer review. I learned that without a good sense of how an audience receives a story, writers may never improve their craft. I also learned how to give valuable advice, which, upon reflection, may have been the most helpful lesson of all. When detecting and verbalizing solutions to areas in need of attention in my peers' writing, I ultimately increased my own writing skills and deepened my cognitive understanding of the writing process.

Perhaps in my initial years of teaching writing to college students, my own difficult experiences with peer review subconsciously directed my lessons. When it came time in the writing process for students to share their work with peers, I invariably started implementing peer review by sharing the story of my experience as a way of connecting to anyone who might be feeling as I had felt. I am passionate about encouraging students to increase their level of trust in themselves and in their peers, to have confidence in their own perspectives and opinions, and to discover positive and successful strategies for collaborating with others. This passion has motivated me to search for strategies that support students' sense of trust—in themselves and in their peers—as well as their psychological safety during the peer review process.

Cynthia received a master of arts in English from Trinity College. She is currently pursuing her PhD at the University of Massachusetts, Lowell. In 2021, Cynthia received the National Institute for Staff and Organizational Development (NISOD) Excellence in Teaching Award. Her most recent paper presentations include "No Expectations Are Low Expectations? Comparing Educational Attainment Among Students With High, Low, or Noncommittal Expectations," presented at the 2021 American Educational Research Association (AERA) Conference, and "Renegotiating Identity: Changing Narratives of Self-Hood and Student Attainment," presented at the 2020 UMass Lowell Virtual Student Research & Community Engagement Symposium. Cynthia's next UDL challenge involves completing her dissertation, which builds upon UDL principles and practices by bringing social and emotional learning (SEL) pedagogy to higher education.

Chapter 10
Randy Laist

Annotated? Overrated: Rethinking Research

As an English teacher for many years, I have developed a repertoire of convincing arguments about the value of writing as a tool for communicating and thinking. In class, I will generally seize on any opportunity to evangelize on behalf of the written word, and while there is a certain amount of ulterior motivation in these spiels (I want students to feel that my class is worth their time and money), they are rooted in sincere personal conviction. I have always gravitated toward books and words, writing has opened a lot of doors for me personally, and I harbor what I think is an objectively reasonable suspicion that literacy plays an instrumental role in human beings' ability to build on the past and move into the future. As with all true believers, however, there is something reflexive and unreflective about my worldview, and so it came as a delightful jolt when, in the wake of one of my eloquent sermons on the value of the written word, one of my students conciliated me by saying, "I know writing is very important to you." I was with him for the first six words, but the last two words struck a strange nerve and provoked me into reevaluating everything I thought I knew.

I should say at this point that this student is one with whom I had worked very closely in a previous class. Zeke self-identifies as neuroatypical, and he delights in problematizing the received truths of the "neurotypical" world, which he does regularly with impish brashness. In our roles as English student and English teacher, our working relationship has usually consisted of him expressing some fascinating perspective on social reality, and me trying to cajole him to put his ideas into writing. When he writes, he writes with insight and wit, but he experiences "obstacles to success" in his interface with word-processing equipment. At the time of his infamous comment, we were discussing an essay about ableist assumptions in accessibility discourse that he had handwritten across five sheets of paper. Zeke's essay, as usual, included insightful critiques, but it was clearly a draft and, as any English teacher would say, would benefit from various revisions. Moreover, since the class itself was a class on writing for publication, a digital version of Zeke's text would allow him to submit it to an accessibility-related journal or magazine. We discussed apps that convert handwriting to digital text, and when Zeke exhibited some ambivalence about using these apps, I volunteered to read his essay into a voice-to-text app as a simple way of getting his words into a digital format that we could then play around with and disseminate. Zeke expressed the objection that the results of this process would be "inauthentic." I was guardedly sympathetic to this concern but offered a few of my own ideas about the advantages of digital text as a writing tool: the way it allows you to manipulate the shape and sequence of ideas, and I think I even said something (to Zeke, who is legally blind) about the way the "visuo-spatial arrangement" of words on a screen can help writers understand their own ideas more clearly. It was at this point that Zeke told me, "I know writing is very important *to you.*"

Was it true? Was all of my thinking on this completely subjective? Was it the case that writing is not really important in an objective, transcendent sense but has only taken on that aura as a result of my own experience and perspective? I was reminded of the principle that "neurons that fire together wire together," as neuropsychologist Donald Hebb put it. Assuming that to be the case, decades of experience as an English teacher and as a word person have ensured that the architecture of my own brain is likely wired to favor writing, making it part of my consciousness and identity. I suspected that this is the way it is with anyone who specializes in any particular area of human endeavor, which means that it is the way for just about every neurotypical adult. We become shaped by the things we do in a way that skews our objective perception of that thing. This is not necessarily bad. It is good that there are people out there expressing the value that "writing is important," just as it is important that there are people out there saying the same thing about math, history, and cryptozoology. Our collective obsessions merge into the meta-mind that is human civilization. All of these ideas, in vague outline, occurred to me in a burst as soon as I heard Zeke's sentence. It also occurred to me that I was having a UDL moment and that this conundrum was an opportunity to reexamine the basic questions of what the goals of a writing class—and of writing itself—are, what it means to "publish" something, and most importantly, what it would take to arrange the class in a way that empowered Zeke to be Zeke, while also challenging him to be the best Zeke he can be.

A full discussion of the way we approached all of these questions is beyond the scope of this chapter, but the upcoming assignment on the syllabus provided an easy opportunity for us to play around with "multiple means" of achieving the assignment goals. In my design of the class, unit four was a week devoted to conducting background research for the articles and presentations the students were preparing. The goal of the unit was pretty straightforward: They had to accumulate information about their topics in order to write about them in a well-informed way. At the same time, however, as is usually the case, this main goal intermingled with ancillary goals—I wanted the students to develop their familiarity with academic research, to practice reading academic articles, and of course, to write, write, write—and the Frankenstein result of all of these mashed-up elements was next week's assignment: the annotated bibliography.

Now don't get me wrong. I love the annotated bibliography, and many students do, too. The annotated bibliography is a rigorous format for compiling and assessing research sources. The researcher records the citation, writes a brief paragraph summarizing the point of view expressed in the source, and responds to the article with an evaluation of its applicability to the researcher's own research project. When I was in graduate school, the process of compiling an annotated bibliography made me feel like I was able to get my mind around what otherwise seemed like a sprawling and incoherent nebula of scholarship relating to my dissertation topic. Having assigned annotated bibliographies to students for many years, I have seen some students fall in love with compiling annotated bibliographies, finding, in some cases, I think, the same kind of empowerment I found. Of course, there have always been other students who have significantly less profound experiences with the annotated bibliography assignment, and then there was Zeke. Zeke was not going to write an annotated bibliography. At the same time, he is a brilliant and prolific researcher. And in any event, whereas other research-writing classes might insist on the value of teaching annotated bibliographies for their own sake, as a form of writing with which any academic researcher should be familiar, this was a class in publication, where the annotated bibliography was intended to be a means to an end, rather than the end itself. This assignment would be a good place to start Zeke-ifying the learning environment.

As in any UDL-informed intervention, I began by identifying the central purpose of the assignment, which, in this case, was simply to create the conditions that would incentivize students to gather information about their research topics. It occurred to me that this goal involved three components that correspond with the three UDL axes of Engagement, Representation, and Action and Expression.

- Engagement: Even students who enjoy compiling annotated bibliographies would likely agree that this particular style of assignment is not as engaging as it might be. Indeed, part of the function of the annotated bib assignment has always been to "enforce" engagement by requiring the students to use writing to detail their involvement with the source. In the context of Zeke's class, it was obvious that a much more authentic form of engagement would be one that allowed students to act as each other's audience. A show-and-tell-style presentation of information from their research sources would not only allow students to have a specific audience in mind as they prepared to discuss their findings but would also provide opportunities for students to discuss their research process, to receive feedback and suggestions from the class, and to spitball strategies for spinning these findings into possible publications.

- Representation: In a more traditional research-writing course, the most privileged sources of information tend to be peer-reviewed research papers from the university library's academic and professional databases. For the publication class, however, while such articles might contain useful facts and perspectives, they were likely to be too specialized to be useful to these student-writers. At the same time, our class discussions had produced many instances of students bringing in information from less "traditional" research sources, including multimedia sources, works of fiction, and interpersonal communication. While Zeke himself navigates professional databases with fluency, I thought it might facilitate a more open-ended discussion about the many ways writers gather information if I invited the students to consult a range of different kinds of sources of information.

▎ Action and Expression: The show-and-tell format replaces the writing assignment with a more dialogical means of demonstrating what they have learned from their research process, and it also allows for a visual or tactile element, since I invite students to bring their research sources into the class, either in the form of hard copies of their sources or of digital links or images. Providing instructions about how students should organize their show-and-tell presentations allowed me to isolate very specific "deliverables" that I wanted students to home in on. In this context, the most important outcomes were that students could identify the main point expressed in each source and could mine the source for interesting factoids and quotes that they might be able to use in their writing projects. I also thought it would be helpful to ask the students to think about the sources themselves from the perspective of potential contributors. If students could answer these four questions about each source, it didn't really matter if they wrote their answers out in complete sentences, provided targeted bullet points in their PowerPoint slides, or improvised their way through their presentation. They were encouraged to present this information in whatever format made the most sense to them.

The assignment instructions were as follows:

Annotated? Overrated: Rethinking Research

This week, we want to dive a little deeper into your research topics. As we continue to develop expertise in our research fields, it becomes helpful to familiarize ourselves with the different sources of information about the things we want to learn about.

Step 1: Identify three different sources of information about your topic. You might consider consulting any of the following sources:

- Professional research journals

- Popular/general-audience magazines

- Articles from online or print-based newspapers

- Journalistic podcasts or television series

- Websites/social media pages

- Nonfiction books

- Documentaries/online videos

- Works of fiction

- Human beings (interview subjects)

- Other (?)

You are welcome to choose three sources from the same category, but you might have a richer research experience if you consider choosing sources from a few different categories.

Step 2: In a PowerPoint document, share a link to each source (or whatever other identifying information might apply). If it is easier, you can bring a "hard copy" of the source (a printout of an article you read, a DVD that you watched, a copy of a book you read, etc.) to class. Then, prepare answers to the following questions:

- Question 1: What is the "main point" expressed in the source?

- Question 2: What is the most interesting piece of information you found in this source?

❭ Question 3: Identify an interesting "pull quote" from the source.

❭ Question 4: In what kind of publication did this source appear, who is their audience, and (if applicable) do they accept unsolicited submissions for publication?

Depending on what works better for you, you may write out answers to these questions in your PowerPoint slides, prepare notes for yourself, or simply do it all in your head.

Step 3: Share your research with the class next time we meet.

The most successful outcome of this revised lesson proved to be the robust class discussion that ensued when the students presented their research to one another. Although the priority in redesigning the assignment was to encourage Zeke to participate as fully as possible, I had also hoped that fostering a more interactive approach would be motivational for the class as a whole, and indeed, all of the students seized the opportunity that the presentations gave them to talk more expansively about their research questions, to debate the utility and reliability of different kinds of sources of information, and to brainstorm suggestions for further inquiry. Most importantly for the purposes of this particular class, inviting the students to bring in digital or hard copies of sources they had consulted allowed us to navigate around within these publications in search of information about how to "talk back" to these sources by submitting our own pieces for publication. The resulting conversation allowed every student in the class to identify at least one publication that solicited the kind of articles that they might potentially write, establishing a clear writing agenda for the coming weeks. When the students were released from the hidebound parameters of a formal annotated bibliography, their research spilled out into a number of stimulating and unpredictable directions, embodying more authentically the multidimensional and improvisational nature of intellectual inquiry.

As for Zeke, eliminating the stumbling block of a formal written assignment allowed him to contribute his unique gifts for research and originality to the class discussion. Although he did not prepare a PowerPoint deck, his descriptions of the content of his sources (three peer-reviewed research articles) rivalled any of his other classmates' for thoroughness and critical analysis. The depth of his familiarity with the sources he discussed provided a model of scholarly engagement, and when other students were presenting their research, Zeke took on the role of co-instructor, asking the students penetrating, detail-oriented questions about the information they extracted from their sources, and emailing his fellow students links to other sources of information about their various topics. Zeke's contributions in this regard were consistently astute, relevant, and helpful, winning him the sincere gratitude of his classmates and reinforcing his own sense of self-efficacy as both a researcher and a colleague. Whereas the "obstacle" of a formal annotated bibliography would likely have exiled Zeke from the class activity, creating a more Zeke-friendly version of the assignment allowed him to demonstrate his unique talents in a way that enriched the entire learning environment for all of the students and for me as well.

This small lesson exemplifies several aspects of why UDL can be such an effective pedagogical framework. For one thing, my efforts to redesign this assignment to make it accessible for Zeke resulted in an assignment that is more accessible for all learners and, consequently, more impactful. This anecdote dramatically illustrates the UDL slogan that "What is good for some is good for all." At the same time, thinking about this lesson in terms of multiple means of engagement, representation, and expression encouraged me to think about the goal of the assignment in a more open-ended way that actually reflects more accurately the real-world nature of academic research projects. In retrospect, an annotated bibliography is clearly suited to a 20th-century context of print media, while the multimedia approach of our UDL-based show-and-tell format seems more appropriate for the internet-based styles of research that prevail in the 21st century. This observation leads me to what is perhaps the most vital contribution that UDL can make to any educator's portfolio of skills: the fact that consistently applying UDL principles requires constant innovation and reevaluation of pedagogical practice, at both the microscale level of individual lesson plans and the macroscale level of "What are we really doing here?" kinds of questions.

These are big questions, of course, and this lesson is, in fact, kind of a cheat, since as I mentioned before, it's an easy example of both an unnecessarily cumbersome "obstacle" (the annotated bibliography) that can be eliminated, as well as a highly flexible goal (do research) that can be achieved in more interesting ways. Now that our research unit is over, Zeke and I have to resume our more difficult conversation about his writing. Zeke cleverly pointed out to me at one point that "this isn't a writing class—it's a publication class," and it is likely that Zeke and I will explore other ways of circumventing traditional English composition, for example, by getting him "published" in the form of a podcast and/or video lecture, but I have not given up on pushing Zeke to expand the role of writing among his repertoire of self-expressive modalities. Inspired and guided by UDL principles, we will continue our collaborative attempt to isolate the relevant barriers—both Zeke's and mine—and to overcome them.

How I Got Here

Randy Laist

I recall very distinctly a Signet paperback edition of *Moby-Dick*, crammed onto a packed bookshelf in the downtown Salvation Army. Twenty-five cents. I had never read *Moby-Dick* at the time, but I knew it had a reputation for being the big one—the epic adventure of human existence, full of profound wisdom and mystery. And here it was on a shelf for 25 cents. And joining it on the shelf: a Pelican *Hamlet*, a Pocket Library edition of *The Decameron*, the Bible, for crying out loud, all similarly priced. All of the world's accumulated wisdom, available for the price of a can of soda.

Something about this memory from my early teens sticks with me. Now, when I think about my decades of experience as an English teacher, I think about the wonder, the happy surprise, of seeing that bookshelf, which consisted primarily of a two-part revelation. One half of this revelation was the sense of how powerful writing is, that it can concentrate the most significant and most inscrutable human knowledge into a sheaf of paper that can fit inside a large pocket. The other half of this revelation involved the sense that this knowledge was so accessible. All you need to get at this information is some spare change and some basic literacy skills. It seemed like the ultimate hack, like I had discovered that the keys to the kingdom had been hidden in plain sight, on an abandoned shelf in a used-stuff store. When I finally read my 25-cent copy of *Moby-Dick*, I probably understood about 10% of it, but the 10% I understood made me want to understand more.

My inspiration as a teacher is to simulate a similar experience for my students, to show them that knowledge is all around them, that language opens doors, and that their own writing presents an opportunity for their perspectives to join the voices that crowd the used-book shelf of history. As I mention in my chapter, sometimes my graphophilia gets the best of me, and I have to remind myself

-115-

that the written word is only one of many means of self-expression. My ongoing UDL challenge is to make self-expression more accessible to more people and to encourage students to use their own words and voices to multiply the number of books (and videos, digital documents, MP3 files, etc.) on our species' collective shelf.

Randy received his doctorate in American literature from the University of Connecticut. He has taught in middle schools, high schools, and colleges, and his writing has appeared in the New York Times, Salon, *and the* Chronicle of Higher Education. *He is the author, most recently, of* The Twin Towers in Film: A Cinematic History of the World Trade Center.

Chapter 11

Phillip J. Fox

Badges and Paths: Creating Learner-Centered Environments in Online Classes

Online learning has played an increasingly critical role in higher education recently, and the design of online courses can determine whether students find the educational materials accessible or frustrating, intuitive or confusing, engaging or bewildering. At Goodwin University, faculty have collaborated with our Center for Teaching Excellence and the Online Studies department in well-intentioned efforts to simplify the process of online learning for students. For example, in online courses, we have created a standardized course menu that contains uniform items such as announcements, syllabus and policies, weekly units, discussions, calendar, a library link, and a gradebook link. We have created a standard approach to 15-week (full semester) and 7.5-week (half semester, accelerated) courses. We have created course calendars that describe weekly due dates and units, and we have stressed the value of standard assignments, due every week, such as discussion board questions, quizzes, and periodic writing assignments. We have made these standards part of a "master" course that is copied at the beginning of the term to all other sections of the same course. The guiding philosophy behind this standardization is the assumption that if students are familiar with the basic layout of a course, they will be more comfortable with the basic layout of many courses and, thus, their uncertainty and anxiety will be minimized. If there is only one road, we have assumed, no one will get lost.

One of the most important elements of Universal Design for Learning, however, is its emphasis on learner variability. When curriculum and pedagogical shifts brought on by UDL arrived at Goodwin, I often found myself wondering, Is our singular approach to managing courses on the learning management system best for all students? I had read some literature on "gamification" and "badging," and inspired by the UDL principle that providing students with different options could be a powerful way of recruiting student interest, I wanted to design a course that emphasized student choice and highlighted the opportunity to earn individual recognition for competency-based achievements. In addition, thinking about the importance that UDL practice places on self-regulation, I wanted to help students determine the pace of the course for themselves. I also considered the possibility that an online course could be designed in a way that provides options for how students perceive course content and that grants opportunities for them to implement executive function strategies. The outcome of these efforts has been a Composition and Literature course that looks very different from many of the other online classes offered at my university but that has nevertheless proven to be very popular with our students.

Engagement: Recruiting Interest

To me, the most meaningful strategy for recruiting student interest is promoting learner choice. I took two specific actions to return a level of choice to the online classroom and to engage students in the course content. First, I questioned one of the existing course goals. One of the original goals in the class was to "write a paper that applies a literary theory to 'The Lottery.'" With all apologies to Shirley Jackson fans, what about the students who were not engaged by "The Lottery"? What about the students who are anxious about writing? The purpose of this goal was obviously to encourage the student to practice the application of a literary theory, so I changed "The Lottery" to "a text of their choice," and I eliminated the requirement that students write a paper. The new goal became "apply a literary theory to a text of their choice." My colleagues and I supported this goal by creating a reading list of texts so that students could choose from the list, and we helped them to make a well-informed choice by breaking that list into sublists of specific texts that are recommended for each assignment. Thus, the new goal was written in a universal way, a way that creates access for learners who differ in their approaches to texts.

Second, I created a series of "paths" to the assignment goals. Think of a path as a way to complete the assignment. For example, students can demonstrate their ability to "apply a literary theory to a text of their choice" by creating a composition, creating and posting a video discussion with a friend, or participating in the discussion board with other classmates. As other instructors adopt this course design, they can create new paths and add them to this goal, which restores greater flexibility to the online teacher as well as to the student. The standard we do not change is that every student must successfully complete at least one path to demonstrate that they have reached the goal.

Engagement: Self-Regulation

I am a firm believer in coaching learners to manage their own schedules, and I took one specific action to encourage self-regulation in the redesigned Comp and Lit course. I removed the course schedule, which, as previously stated, was locked into a weekly approach. In its place, I put a series of guidelines for students. I ranked the assignments in the order of the time commitment they typically involve, placing the ones that took the least amount of time at the bottom of the list and those that required the greatest time commitment at the top. As an example, the final class project is ranked at the top, taking the largest amount of time, while the literary terms worksheet, a short assignment, is ranked at the bottom. It is important to note here that I did not specify how much time any assignment should take, because every learner is different. What I did provide is a general guideline. I also set the course to have milestone markers—that is, general announcements of what students might consider completing and by when. The standard we do not change is that every student must successfully complete all the required assignments in the course.

Representation: Perception

A multimodal approach to composition encourages students to think of rhetorical skills as encompassing a broad range of expressive possibilities that includes, but is not limited to, written communication. Thus, we took another action to encourage broad latitude in responding to some assignments in the course. In the original version of the Composition and Literature course, many of the assignments and course resources were text based. For example, the assignment directions were presented through text, the assignment resources were web texts, and the assignments themselves called for writing (as mentioned in the previous course goal). In order to supplement this text-based emphasis with a more multimodal suite of instructional materials, my colleagues and I made videos to introduce assignments, to discuss text annotating, and to explain literary analysis. Of course, we also kept text-based resources such as lecture notes for the students who prefer reading. I also changed some assignments from written papers to audio and video submissions. In some cases, students also have different options for demonstrating that they have met the course goals. The standard of the assignment is the same for all students, but we changed how the content is delivered and handed in.

Action and Expression: Executive Functions

The English content area at Goodwin University espouses a process-based approach to composition, particularly in 100-level courses such as Composition and Literature. To help students set revision goals, I believe in looking at drafts at various stages in a composition process. With that in mind, I took another action in the course rebuild. Since the original course design locked students into a weekly schedule, many students approached each assignment as a "one and done" proposition. They would complete one assignment and turn immediately to the next. By removing the barrier of a weekly schedule, the redesigned course encouraged many students to manage their lives more independently. I doubled down on that idea by building the middle portion of the course and its assignment paths around the idea of revisions. I constructed a statement that read "Revision is a serious part of this course. You cannot earn credit for an assignment until you have earned an 80 or above on the assignment. Assignments scored below an 80 may be revised at any time during the course except in the last unit." In addition, I built the idea of assignment revision into the feedback I provided to students about their work, indicating what a student must revise and how they might revise it. In this way, this course redesign raises the standard for passing, and we help students reach their goals by challenging them to build on their own successes and progressively improve their level of mastery.

Reactions From Students

We have now run this version of Composition and Literature for five semesters and collected over 120 positive student responses to the course layout and features through the once-a-semester online course evaluation platform to which the university asks students to respond. In these responses, students explain how they have become more purposeful, resourceful, and strategic as a result of their engagement with the coursework. One student wrote,

> I was a little nervous at first, but the course layout made it so easy to adjust to this course. I never felt alone or frustrated because I could reach out to my professor who always seemed to be explaining assignments in terms of goals. I always knew why I needed to do something.

What I find particularly impactful here is the student's statement that understanding the goals of the course helped to reduce feelings of abandonment and frustration. Clearly, the design of this course motivated the student and helped them to succeed in the class. Another student wrote,

> This course felt very patient in order to complete the papers that are assigned. I would recommend all students take this course, especially if they have had a hard time understanding what is expected in other courses. This class was very clear.

Again, the student's emphasis on patience and positive emotions vindicated my own goals in redesigning the course, which prioritized the effort to reduce student anxiety and to help students cope with their feelings of uncertainty. Another student wrote,

> This is my second time taking this class. Although I was nervous to take it online for the second time, I'm so glad I got the new version of the course the second time around. My first class I was given a different course and I got little feedback and I was just confused as to what was due when . . . then it was overwhelming to manage each week. This time around I earned an A and appreciated how not every assignment was some massive paper.

The interesting thing in this student's comment is the idea that they repeated the class and found the revised course less confusing and less overwhelming. Most importantly, when we talk about student perception in UDL, the last sentence is enlightening. The student enjoyed the variation in assignments and the customizing of information. Yet another student's comment reiterates this point: "The course is very fair with work, there are suggested due dates, but it lets you work at your own pace to submit the work." In this brief student comment, the student aligns fairness and being treated well with the idea of working at their own pace. Students must believe they are in a fair, safe environment in order to practice coping skills and strategies.

Other student comments provide a window into the challenges faced by online students that might be invisible to their instructors. One student writes,

> This is a challenging time for me, because I am also taking microbiology with a lab online. I have been crying every Sunday since March when I must complete lab assignments and other assignments in other classes on the same night.

> *My one bright spot was this course because I could set my own schedule and work my hardest to obtain a good grade when I had time to.*

I have deep empathy for this student's emotional frustration with weekly assignments in several courses all coming due at the same time and day. Gone are the days where instructors can simply say, "That's college," to every struggling student. It is particularly troubling to see students whose earnest attempts to manage their own schedules and to make their own executive decisions collide with unresponsive and poorly designed instructional routines. Instructors can genuinely help students develop a deeper sense of executive function by meeting them halfway. Another student expresses similar sentiments about the challenges of balancing course assignments with a busy extracurricular life:

> *The first time I used online learning I was taking my classes while traveling for work. It was hard to manage but that was due to my busy schedule and the way all of the courses had due dates on the same day. This course makes it very easy for online learning and I appreciate how I could schedule around my job and take a day off if I needed to.*

Many of the students who attend Goodwin balance their academic work with full-time jobs. It is rewarding to see that a student can manage the stress of the workweek and school week due, in part, to the course's flexibility.

Finally, one student's comment demonstrates how motivated they were to share their feedback about the class:

> *OK, so I rated intellectually demanding as agree instead of strongly agree, but please don't make the class any more demanding! I rate it this because I feel I am 100% capable of meeting the class's demands, however it is still time consuming. The literature that has been chosen is quite*

> *different and confusing, at least for me, and requires a lot of re-reading and time to dissect the text before I feel like I comprehend it. I also absolutely love the badge earning layout of this class as this allows me to move at my own pace, which reduces a lot of the anxiety I have associated with being pressured to meet specific deadlines. I am awful at meeting deadlines and this greatly affects my grades because I end up usually handing things in late, so I very much prefer the freedom this badge layout grants me. I also feel like this freedom allows me to learn better because I'm not just rushing through assignments in a poor attempt to meet the due date, rather I have the time to actually pay attention and learn. For the first time ever I can say I'm actually enjoying an English class, which is a subject I have always detested. I would certainly recommend this class.*

There is a wealth of information that comes from this student's experiences with the course. The student recognizes the course is demanding but completable—right in the sweet spot for a course that will push a student to learn. The student recognizes that the course layout requires learners to manage their time effectively. Perhaps the most empowering element in the student's reflection and commentary is the recognition that anxiety can be associated with pressure, rushing through, and failing. Anxiety can be encouraging as well as incapacitating. In this case, the student found the course provided just enough anxiety to be motivational, propelling them to complete the coursework. Universal Design for Learning certainly accentuates the educational value of varying demands and optimizing challenges.

Students Respond

We have built a course based on UDL principles, and students are responding. Students respond to a course that is purposeful, and they are motivated by the freedom to manage their time in a way that best benefits them. Students respond to a course that accurately represents what they must do and that allows them the opportunity to do that work in different, creative ways, putting them in charge of their learning. Students respond to a course that is goal directed and mastery oriented.

The next time you are designing or redesigning a course, ask yourself: What is the easiest way for me to check my own egotism? What is the fastest way for me to see things from a student's perspective? How can I be a partner in removing barriers in content and curriculum for all students? Universal Design for Learning helps us answer these questions. Course changes can be powerful when they are informed by an educational philosophy that puts students at the center of the learning process and that celebrates their personal freedom to forge their own paths.

How I Got Here

Phillip J. Fox

Here are some of the most important facts that no one needs to know about Phil Fox.

Without offending anyone who writes about cats, I dream of writing about cats, a lot. But I mostly chicken out and write things like this article; or *Discover the Writer in You*, a textbook about writing; or "Fake News and Family," an article in *Successes and Setbacks of Social Media*.

One of my favorite movies is *13 Going on 30*; I feel like that every day, and I am way, way, way past 30. I have three children. Two are under the age of three, and I wish I lived in Daniel Tiger's neighborhood. But I really live in Lyme, Connecticut, as a deer-tick ninja. I graduated from Connecticut College where many of my professors wore bow ties and tweed caps while smoking pipes by the fireside. I hold a PhD in educational leadership; sometimes, I hold it at night, when no one is around except Trouble the cat, and it is 3 am, and I am eating the last bag of Oreos, scrolling through my student loan balance sheet while practicing what my therapist calls "healthy" crying.

I devote the rest of my time to teaching writing and information literacy as the director of English at Goodwin University. I teach those topics to anyone who shows up for class, or students in the hallway, or shoppers at Walmart, or that bearded fellow who rides a bike through town every day at 12 pm.

Universal Design for Learning is a challenge for me as an educator. It is a challenge to wake up every day—after all those Oreos—and think of different ways to make curriculum accessible to all students. I am committed to a future of UDL in all classes, and my next UDL challenge is helping bring UDL to each English and writing course.

In addition to acting as director of English at Goodwin University, Phillip has also served as the president of faculty senate and as the assistant coach for the men's basketball team. In his downtime, he likes woodworking, basketball, and playing guitar. Keep an eye out for his cat book.

Careers

Chapter 12

Keith A. Carter

Go-Karts and Arc Welders: Simulating Our Way to Success in a UDL-Informed Welding Class

As a naval master training specialist, I designed and taught courses in naval nuclear and non-nuclear power-plant welding and naval leadership and development. In my current "assignment" as a professor of welding, I use many of the same instructional techniques with my manufacturing students that I mastered in the navy. When I encountered Universal Design for Learning, I recognized right away that the learner-centered framework it provided could be implemented to enhance a competency-based welding program. We expect that students will develop a complete understanding of the various welding processes. In our program, UDL-inspired innovations have helped students to reach this goal and to increase their levels of proficiency. With the growing demand for skilled workers in the manufacturing career fields, it is certainly worthwhile to consider how UDL methodologies can be implemented to enhance the effectiveness and accessibility of manufacturing training programs.

Welding is the joining of two metal pieces through coalescence, the process of heating them to temperatures that cause fusion. The teaching of welding can be a bit tricky, depending on the methodology used. The instructional design often creates a barrier that stunts student achievement and creates frustration and considerable material waste. Typically, the new welding student is placed in the lab with a piece of metal, a stinger or rod holder, a welding rod, and a machine. The instructor and student are decked out in the welding gear, and the student nervously hears the instructor's voice as they explain how to strike an arc properly. Upon brushing or tapping the end of the 7018 electrodes against the base material, the arc, a bright fireball of intense heat and light, will form. Once the arc is established using one of the two methods, the instructor will begin to run a bead.

Barriers to Learning

The students are hampered by two obvious barriers. The first barrier is the difficulty of seeing the instructor's nearly imperceptible motions as the weld arc is established. The second is the challenge of hearing the instructor as they speak about maintaining the arc while talking into a welding helmet. When the student tries to replicate the instructor's actions, they are usually not comfortable. Their welding electrode invariably sticks to the metal, which causes them to fight the electrode as they attempt to remove it from the plate. The aggressive pulling on the electrode to dislodge it causes the protective coating or flux to break away and off the electrode, and the electrode at this point is useless. Material usage can become costly if the instructors do not provide the necessary one-on-one instruction.

Several other identifiable barriers also hinder student learning in the welding classroom. Faculty have discussed the challenge of teaching the different work angles and speeds associated with welding as presented in our curriculum. Before students entered the lab, we used PowerPoints and whiteboard drawings to illustrate the use of the lead angle, but we noted that this instructional method was not effective. The same problem reappeared with the teaching of work angles and speed of travel. When hired by the university, I noticed two virtual welders in the classroom. I was not a fan of using welding simulators to teach welding. I was skeptical that a simulator could ever be a substitute for the physical experience of learning to weld. Before starting the first welding program at Goodwin University, I was indifferent to the use of simulators and suggested we not waste time with them. Nevertheless, I made an effort to figure out how to use them. But I was still stumped by the challenge of how to incorporate virtual welding simulators into the curriculum. After days of playing with the virtual welders in the various weld positions, I struggled to imagine how students would use them and what role they would play in the program.

The UDL Connection

Then, I made a UDL connection. I thought about my daughter, who, in kindergarten, convinced me to purchase a go-kart for her sixth birthday. She had strict requirements regarding what components this go-kart should have. These components included a roll cage, key start, horn, and headlights. At the time of purchase, I did not realize that she was using the go-kart as a simulator to learn how to drive. When she turned 13 and had outgrown her go-kart, I suggested replacing it with a larger go-kart. To my surprise, she told me that the only reason she needed a go-kart was so that she could learn how to drive, so when she turned 16, there would be no reason for her not to get a car and her driver's permit.

Did the simulation work? Yes. The go-kart scaffolded her learning, allowing her to practice core skills in a low-stakes environment and to develop confidence as a driver. It also allowed her to be in the "driver's seat" of her own learning process, developing new skills and habits in her own way and at her own pace. Could a similar process help my students master the similarly hands-on skill of welding?

Adopting New Methods

The UDL approach encouraged me to consider adopting new learning methods into my teaching in order to remove the instructional barriers that were complicating my welding students' path to mastery. We decided to include the welding simulators and videos in our curriculum before entering the welding lab. The inclusion of this new resource reflects the UDL principle of providing students with multiple means of representing instructional information, since the "virtual" gamer experience provided by the welding simulator complements the "theoretical" experience provided by lectures and video tutorials. The combination of showing students the videos and giving them chances to use the welding simulators before they entered our welding labs turned out to result in unbelievable success. With the help of the practice they were getting with the simulator, our students were learning to strike an arc and run a weld bead properly. This accelerated progress reduced costs associated with wasted materials. As fascinating as it may sound, we have consistently watched this process repeated with successive cohorts of students. The sticking of welding electrodes was limited to a small number of occurrences, which were easily corrected by the program's instructional team.

We also used UDL principles to incorporate the welding simulators into the course of study in a meaningful way. First, the students are given a mock coupon for a welding task. Second, students use a procedure sheet associated with the welding coupon. The students are tested on their ability to read the procedure sheet and the simulator's correct setup. Third, once correctly set up, the simulator provides a simulated lab environment. The electrode and electrode holder simulate the weld electrode's fusion into the base metal as the student is welding. Fourth, the computer program provides the students with information about the work, lead angles, and arc distance. These simulations are also assisted by the simulated sounds that replicate those typically produced during welding operations. Finally, the simulator identifies, tracks, and scores attributes, leading to better welds. In essence, the students learn what they are doing wrong and what they need to correct during the simulated welding process.

The UDL-inspired implementation of welding simulators into our program has provided solutions for at least three chronic challenges in welding instruction. The simulators help students learn to start or strike an arc in a way that eliminates material waste. Experience with the simulator also allows students to feel more confident when they enter an actual welding lab. They are less anxious, their self-efficacy is high, and they are self-motivated to learn. Third, the simulator is used as a training tool. The students learn what the lead angle is, what the working angle is, and how to use a tight arc or to prevent long arcing. The information can be presented in the traditional classroom, but UDL simulators create an immersive learning environment that enhances the learning process.

Universal Design for Learning "provides the opportunity for all students to access, participate in, and progress in the general-education curriculum by reducing barriers to instruction" (Ralabate, 2011). In a UDL-informed environment, students use instructional time for learning, rather than negotiating the red tape of a traditional one-size-fits-all instructional process. This is what makes UDL an exciting innovation in training, especially in the manufacturing field. In its emphasis on learner variability, UDL also supports equality and accessibility in education, opening opportunities for underserved populations of students. Welding students tend to have unique backgrounds that differentiate them from students in more academic college programs. They tend to be people who are not interested in white-collar careers or the four-year professional pathways to those careers. Welding students prefer to work with their hands. They are interested in short training programs that lead to jobs that pay a fair wage. Like most manufacturing careers, welding is one of those careers that often provides second-chance careers for the underrepresented. UDL provides an educational perspective that disrupts traditional academic practice, inspiring new instructional methods capable of connecting with students from all backgrounds and across widely diverse disciplines.

From Go-Kart to VW Beetle

My objection to the use of welding simulators was rooted in tradition and in my previous experiences teaching welding. I did not see how a welder could be taught to weld using a video simulator. How wrong was I for thinking inside the traditional box? The simulators used in the welding program at GU have turned out to be essential components of the program. The students are achieving skills in the classroom that baffle our instructors and our lab tech, who continues to ask the question, "Have they welded before they came here?" This question is provoked by the students' ability to enter the lab and lay close-to-certifiable beads on their first project. The response to the question is always no. They have not; this is their first time.

In 2020 my daughter turned 16. I purchased her a Volkswagen Beetle three months before her birthday. On the eve of her birthday, my wife and I surprised her with the car. But the surprise was on us when she took the car into a large parking lot and drove around as if she had been driving for years. She navigated the directional line in the parking lot without hesitation or disruption. Her first real road test was even more surprising. As she drove the car, I recall sitting in the passenger seat and relaxing as she transformed her simulated experiences into real mastery.

How I Got Here

Keith A. Carter

I was born and reared in Houma, Louisiana, where I joined the U.S. Navy, and I am currently a resident of Oakdale, Connecticut. I am an assistant professor and program manager for the welding programs at Goodwin University, School of Business Management and Manufacturing. I also serve as the CEO and founder of Holistic Education Mentoring and Development; co-CEO and cofounder of Inspire Center for Diversity, Equity, Inclusion, and Belonging; and a founding member of Many Mentors. I served our nation honorably for 23 years of U.S. Navy service, a career highlighted by expertise in organizational leadership and development, project management, counseling, safety and security management, program coordination, and career advisement.

My work as a community-based educational specialist has focused on minority youth mentoring and program development. I also work as a life coach, motivational speaker, and inspirational leader. In the past years, I have worked tirelessly to find opportunities to create social change and develop educational programming to increase academic achievement and college awareness for underserved communities of color. I am also a founder of the Net 21 youth program. This was a collaboration between Holistic Mentoring Education and Development, the U.S. Coast Guard, and New London NAACP that functioned to increase diversity and awareness in cybersecurity career fields for underserved minority middle school children.

I answered the call to serve my church community, was ordained as a deacon in 2019, and am also a founding member of the SOAR Ministry.

Keith has earned a master's of science in human relations from the University of Oklahoma, Norman; a master's of science in social work from the University of Connecticut; a master's of science in psychology from Walden University; a bachelor's of science in workforce education and development from the University of Southern Illinois, Carbondale; post-master's certifications in online psychology instruction from Walden University; a certificate in Black ministries from the Hartford Seminary; a health leadership fellowship from the Connecticut Health Foundation; a teaching fellowship in Universal Design for Learning from Goodwin College; a Six Sigma Yellow Belt; and a certification as a naval master training specialist in classroom instruction, group facilitation, and curriculum design. Since his retirement, he has worked in higher education and developmental training. He has dedicated the more significant portion of his time to mentoring and expanding diversity and educational opportunities in the healthcare and STEM professions. Keith is a doctoral candidate in educational psychology at Walden University.

Chapter 13

Karrie Morin

UDL and the Freedom to Fail: Technology, Games, Innovation, and Play

learned early on the importance of risk-taking and failure in the classroom. I believe that true learning takes place when barriers are removed and when students feel safe to try new things. Students need a supportive and engaging environment where they are motivated to push themselves beyond their original expectations. Therefore, I made that my first goal in my classroom. I was determined to provide a safe and secure classroom environment to allow my students the freedom to take risks and the freedom to fail. UDL became the backbone of my classroom and my curriculum.

I have always allowed my students to express themselves naturally and allowed discussions to flow organically. The early childhood education course I teach, ECE 320, Education and Technology, was no exception. This course was designed to familiarize future teachers with all of the different technologies available for an early childhood classroom. The students are given the opportunity to design a classroom curriculum where technology is an essential component for both the teacher and the children. There were so many possibilities. I reviewed the learning outcomes and previous course curricula. I began reading all the books and started preparing an engaging and content-rich learning environment for my students. I developed the curriculum using multiple modes of media to explain concepts, and I provided real world, hands-on experiences. My goal was becoming a reality. I was creating an engaging, technology-rich classroom that was also a safe and secure learning environment for my students. At the start of class on day one, I told my students that it was my first time teaching this ECE 320 course. I set the stage for them. I explained to them that I wanted to experiment and try new things, I wanted to take chances, and I wanted a secure environment in which to do so. I wanted to be creative and not only to think outside the box but to remove the box completely!

So, this is how we began. Each week, I provided a technology-rich curriculum explaining the importance of teaching technology in the digital age. I further explained that the technology does not and should not drive the lesson. (My colleagues hear me say this all the time.) I started to teach my students the benefits of using technology and the appropriate use of technology at specific ages, especially for young children, prekindergarten through age 8. Throughout the course, I was always working to keep the question "What is age appropriate?" in the forefront of our minds. I designed various learning experiences, which included not only lectures and discussions but also experimentation, trial and error, group activities, lab time, and reflection. I did not simply teach the new technology; I taught them how to use the new technology in their own classroom.

Throughout the semester, we discussed the many benefits of using technology with young children. I incorporated the use of digital images and photography to emphasize key components, to provide opportunities for scientific exploration, and to demonstrate the process of inquiry. Some of the key assignments included designing blogs, creating digital stories, organizing documentation panels, designing makerspaces, and incorporating QR codes into the lessons. I taught digital literacy, information literacy, and innovation. A couple of weeks into the semester, I had developed a great relationship with my students. I encouraged them to share their ideas, stories, projects, and presentations, and they felt comfortable doing so. Our classroom became a supportive learning environment where each person was respectful of others' thoughts and ideas. There was a lot of conversation throughout the semester, and when it came time to present their projects, they excelled. We were breaking down the barriers so that each student could learn to take risks not only in my ECE 320 classroom but in their own classrooms as well.

Midway through the semester, it was time to try something new. Thinking back on what I had learned from my UDL training, I introduced games and play into our classroom. I became very excited and enthusiastic about this lesson. I incorporated multiple means of representation and engagement to explain my subject matter. I provided many examples, including personal narratives, websites, and videos, to enhance my lecture. By the end of class, not only had my students designed their own games, but we were playing them too. I titled this unit "UDL and the Freedom to Fail: Technology, Games, Innovation, and Play." The goal for this unit was to apply techniques for supporting risk-taking and collaboration in the early childhood classroom. I explained that games and play are excellent ways to encourage risk-taking in young children. Play brings people together and relieves stress. It helps children thrive and focus on creative thinking. I reminded my students that what might not be a risk for one person might be a big risk for another.

I started class by showing the video "Play Is Necessary," a talk Kevin Carroll gave at TEDx Harlem in 2012. In the talk, Carroll explains the importance of play: "Play is serious business. Play is at the root of creativity, problem-solving, abstract thinking, imagination, and innovation." I love being able to incorporate this TED Talk into this course. Carroll is a powerful and inspirational speaker. As a class, we paused and listened carefully to his words: "Don't talk about it. Be about it." He talked about how important play is, even for adults. I reminded my students that we should play often.

I followed up this advice with guidelines suggested by Taddei and Budhai (2017) to build a safe space for risk. These guidelines include the following:

- Embrace risk-taking as a productive and integral part of the classroom environment in order to encourage children to take risks.

- Help students support and encourage one another to learn something new and share that learning with others.

- Allow time for informal conversations and community and relationship building.

- Model risk-taking behavior by letting your students know you are trying something for the first time.

- If things don't work as planned, use that as a learning opportunity; discuss what happened and what could be done differently.

- Create a fun, engaging environment.

- Build a professional learning community (PLC) to collaborate with other teachers and professionals to develop learning plans.

- Provide time for reflection.

Next, I introduced the MIT Education Arcade article "Moving Learning Games Forward." As a class, we discussed the role of play and the five freedoms. We focused on the freedom to fail and being allowed that freedom to foster risk-taking and play. Klopfer, Osterweil, and Salen (2009) described the freedom to fail as the idea that

> One doesn't actually fail at play per se, but one is free to do things at play that would look like failure in other contexts. Think of the block tower that inevitably collapses, or the sandcastle fated to disappear with the tide. At play the child has unlimited freedom to undertake such doomed enterprises, and learns as much about the nature of things from failure as from success. Every fall off a skateboard, every crumpled up drawing, every lost game of Candyland is a small failure. Fortunately, children at play don't have adults looming over them, fretting about the cost of these failures, and so children are free to learn from failure and move ever closer to mastery of their world. (p. 4)

My students were intrigued and excited. I asked them to open their laptops or tablets because we were going to play a game. I opened Kahoot! on the SMART Board and showed them the application. I explained that Kahoot! is a web-based game and learning platform that provides students with the opportunity to answer questions in a quick-moving and friendly competition. There are multiple assessment strategies and interactive lessons for students built right within Kahoot!

It was then time to play. We played a quick game of Kahoot! that I created for an early childhood classroom. The lesson was about letters and sounds. My students loved it. They loved the fun competition. I loved listening to their laughter, comments, and exclamations. To continue the engagement and excitement, I introduced the next challenge: to make their own learning game. Their faces changed. They looked apprehensive. I quickly reminded them of the safe environment that we created and the freedom to fail. Then something happened. I was excited, and the students saw my excitement. They saw that I wasn't afraid to fail. Those feelings resonated with my students. They paused and reflected, and they decided to take a chance, to take a risk, and to play.

I started by showing them how to design learning games. I showed them the Kahoot! application and how easy it was to use. I showed them how to add questions, images, and puzzles. I showed them how to make interactive lessons. We discussed the benefits of playing games in an early childhood classroom, which include increased motivation, optimized learning, practice with problem-solving, and enhanced positivity. None of them had ever designed an interactive learning game before. I gave them some time to create their own educational games. I gave them all the resources that they needed, I showed them websites with the best copyright-free images, and I gave them time to reflect on their lessons and on their students. They thought about the lessons they were teaching at that time. They started talking amongst themselves, and I could hear the buzz around the classroom. Every student in my class was engaged, excited, and trying something new. It was fantastic!

My students commented on the fun game-show style. They agreed that Kahoot! was an appropriate application for children ages PK to 8. Educators could use this application to reinforce concepts and ideas that were previously taught. They liked the fact that you could change the speed of the game to make it faster or slower. This could increase the challenge for more advanced learners. Kahoot! is a perfect way to increase student participation, engagement, and motivation. As a class, we discussed some of the barriers to learning that might be associated with this application. In some cases, this game may require adult support. Teachers or parents must be actively involved in the game, especially if students cannot read independently. This game also requires fine motor skills for effective manipulation and navigation of the screen. Once they finished designing their own educational games, we played some of them. Each game was different. One student designed a game about the differences between living and nonliving things. Another student developed a game about the four seasons, specifically focusing on the exploration of spring. My students continued discussing the benefits of each game they created and played. There was a renewed sense of accomplishment throughout the room.

If it wasn't for learning the UDL principles, I never would have tried this lesson. It was the best class that I ever taught. My students were ready to implement games and interactive lessons in their own classrooms. They were thriving, blossoming, energized, and engaged. It was exhilarating to be their teacher. UDL opens up limitless possibilities for both teachers and students, and especially for students who are learning to be teachers and for teachers teaching future teachers.

How I Got Here

Karrie Morin

I come from a family of teachers. I had to be different. When finishing my bachelor's degree many years ago, I had a fleeting thought of becoming a university professor. That is exactly what it was: fleeting. I started my career in information technology in a large corporation. It was a good time to be in that field. I was well respected and proud of all the work that I accomplished as an IT systems engineer. I had a lot of responsibility, building software installation packages and troubleshooting over 300 corporate applications. With this career path, I was able to provide a good life for my son and me. Then everything changed. My company merged with another company, and talks of layoffs followed. After almost 20 years in IT, I lost my job. It was time to make some difficult decisions.

I thought about my life and the goals that I wanted to accomplish. I decided to leave corporate America and go back to school for my master's degree. I found the perfect degree program: MS in educational technology. It paired my love of technology with my newfound love (although I did not know it yet) of teaching! Once I completed my master's degree, I taught at two different universities and fell in love with teaching. About a year later, I secured a full-time position as the coordinator for the Center for Teaching Excellence (CTE) at Goodwin University. With this new position, I was able to teach in multiple ways. I designed faculty professional development programs for the CTE and taught communication courses for the School of Applied Liberal Arts and Social Sciences. It was the best of both worlds. Seeing the many benefits of Universal Design for Learning firsthand, I have continued to incorporate UDL principles into my classroom.

Karrie received her bachelor's degree in communication and her master of science in educational technology from Central Connecticut State University. She loves incorporating her love of UDL with her love of OER (open educational resources). She has received CT Council OER grants for the last two years, saving students over $114,000. Her last presentation about OER was entitled "Goodwin OER: From Imagination to Implementation." When she's not hard at work making life easier for faculty at Goodwin University, she's interviewing UDL fellows in her UDL ERA video series alongside cohost Dana Sheehan. Karrie's next UDL challenge is to make online synchronous courses more engaging for students.

Chapter 14
Michelle Dent

It's the Passion, It's the Motivation—It's the Goal

When I began teaching in the field of early childhood education, things went well in general. I was sure that my continued knowledge acquisition and level of expertise would ensure my success at engaging students and helping them be successful learners. My students were motivated to learn what I was there to teach, and they absorbed the real-world experiences I shared with eagerness and enthusiasm. My classes were full of engaging discussions about the readings and videos we shared, as well as hands-on experiences in which I modeled the ways I hoped my students would engage with the children in their early childhood classrooms.

I struggled, however, with assessing my students' success. Projects, like creating a math game or a creative art experience, usually went well. Asking my students to share their learning by writing reflective essays or synthesis papers was not as successful. Some students were able to express themselves in writing and share their knowledge and competence in the different content areas without difficulty. Other students, however, struggled. The more they were assessed through writing, the more they struggled, and the more they struggled, the less engaged they became. I watched these students lose their enthusiasm for learning and move through courses without motivation. They were in the class to get their degree, not to learn and improve their skills. The light had gone out.

Universal Design for Learning helped me to change the trajectory for these students and turn the light back on. My approach was twofold. First, I needed to find ways to help students who struggled to express themselves in writing be more successful. Other UDL-trained faculty in other disciplines, as well as our wonderful librarians, were instrumental in providing much-needed support. The second part of my approach was to look at the assessments themselves.

While I was participating in the university's UDL professional development program, I was teaching the capstone course for our bachelor's degree program. It was the first time I had taught the course, and the topics and readings were great. The content moved the students from thinking of themselves as teachers to thinking of themselves as early childhood professionals. They came to class excited about the readings and participated eagerly in our discussions and hands-on experiences. Again, the problem was the assessments. In addition to completing other types of assessments, the students were required to write three reading-synthesis papers on different topics for approximately 20% of their total grade. When we went over the syllabus, they did not complain; they were accustomed to being assessed in this way. When I read the first round of papers, the results were as expected. A few of the papers truly demonstrated the students' understanding of the content, other papers demonstrated some understanding, but some of the papers indicated that students did not understand the content. Yet, from working with the students in class, I knew that these students did understand. So why did the assessment not provide an accurate account of their level of understanding?

When I looked at the assessments through the UDL lens, certain indicators stood out to me as problematic. The first issue that was glaringly obvious was that the assessments expected the students to demonstrate their learning by writing a paper, yet none of the course outcomes mentioned any kind of writing proficiency. Furthermore, with 20% of the grade linked to three papers, choice and autonomy were certainly lacking, as was the ability to use multiple media to communicate learning. Finally, the students in this class were passionate about providing high-quality early childhood education and supporting young children and families. Expertise in communicating through formal synthesis papers did not feel relevant, nor did it provide the students with a useful way to transfer the knowledge gained from the readings, class discussions, and hands-on experiences to their professional lives.

For logistical reasons, I chose to look at the third assignment. I knew I needed time to address all of the important indicators I had identified to create an assignment that the students would find engaging and motivating as well as meaningful in that it assessed the intended outcomes. The outcomes being assessed were as follows:

Students will be able to

1. Examine current issues in education, and develop and articulate a position.

2. Synthesize information from reputable sources and cite them using APA.

The topic of the assignment was school readiness. I asked the students to read a scholarly article, a position statement from the National Association for the Education of Young Children, a conceptual framework issued by UNICEF, and a policy issued by the American Academy of Pediatrics. To ensure that all learners could access the information, in addition to the readings, we would also watch a TED Talk on school readiness, analyze the readings in small groups before sharing our findings with the whole group, and share "readiness" stories based on our own experiences with children, families, and schools. I felt comfortable that after engaging with the content in all of these ways, all of the students would be able to understand the concept of school readiness and develop an informed position on the topic. Next, I needed to create an assessment that was authentic and relevant, that provided the students with the ability to choose how to share their learning, and that was tied to the intended outcomes.

When I looked at my roster of students, the answer jumped out at me. They were a cross-section of classroom teachers, paraprofessionals, and program directors. Some were getting their bachelor's degrees and intended to remain in their roles. Others intended to go on for their master's degrees for certification to teach in the public schools. All were passionate about supporting children, families, and the early childhood profession. School readiness is a topic that has been discussed and debated in the field for a long time. It is very important that preschool teachers and administrators understand the topic and can share their understanding with families as well as other professionals. How would they share this vital information? During parent orientation? Perhaps through a newsletter?

In class, it was clear that students came to the conversation with different perspectives based on prior experience. The information we were analyzing required students to reflect on what they thought they knew and to gain perspective on how this analysis pushed them to form new understandings and opinions. The conversation was lively and passionate. Then, toward the end of class, I brought up the assessment and told the students I had made some adjustments. The instructions for the revised assignment were as follows.

Using the assigned readings on school readiness, information shared in class, and your own understanding and thoughts about the topic, reflect on what you have learned, identify themes across the readings and other media, and share your insights, perspectives, and new ideas or understandings about what "school readiness" is and its significance to the young children and families that you work with. Information from all sources should be interwoven with your own ideas to form a cohesive document.

You can share your learning by

1. Writing a 2- to 3-page reading synthesis paper.

2. Writing a newsletter to the families you work with in order to help them understand school readiness and its significance.

3. Preparing a presentation for your colleagues and/or the families you work with on the topic of school readiness.

Please note that if you choose options 2 or 3 and you work with a Spanish-speaking population, you may write in the language of the population you will be writing for or presenting to.

I should note that there were two students in my class whose first language was Spanish, struggled with writing in English, and taught in predominantly Spanish settings. I felt comfortable that my level of Spanish was up to the task of understanding and assessing their work if presented in their native language.

Synthesis Assignment: School Readiness

I also provided the students with the revised rubric, which was linked to the actual outcomes. This new assessment required the students to provide an introduction that shared an overview of the author's position on the topic. It required the students to synthesize the information from various sources into major themes through which they would demonstrate their understanding by summarizing the main ideas and explaining how each supported their expressed point of view. It also required correct spelling, grammar, and APA formatting. It did not, however, require a well-organized paper with an introduction, body paragraphs, and a conclusion.

At first, the students seemed unsure how to respond. I got a lot of questions like "I can write about school readiness in a newsletter? Like the ones I send home every month?" "I can do a PowerPoint presentation?" "Can I include pictures?" By the time the students left class that night, they seemed to understand the options. Some were even smiling and talking as they waited for the elevator about what they might do. I was hopeful that providing options for how to demonstrate their understanding in ways that were relevant to their professional lives would create a path to success for all of the students in the class. Now, I just had to wait and see if I was right!

I was very encouraged with the results of the revised assignment. From the 14 students in the class, I received 5 papers, 6 newsletters, and 3 PowerPoint presentations. Not all used perfect spelling, grammar, or APA format, but all of the students were able to demonstrate their understanding of the topic using the information from the various readings and media to explain their position on school readiness. Much to my disappointment, no one submitted their assignment in Spanish. When I asked one of the native Spanish speakers about this, she explained that she cannot write well in either language, a struggle faced by many bilinguals who had their native language torn away from them when they entered school. A difficult issue but, alas, a subject for a different paper.

As a follow-up, during our next class together after the assignment was due, I asked the students to reflect on their feelings about the assignment revision. They wrote words like excited, happy, empowered, useful, and meaningful. I also asked them to tell me if they believed they had met the outcomes, which I had written in big letters across the whiteboard in the front of the room. They all said yes, with big smiles on their faces. As I looked at those faces, I realized that for all of the students, the light was back on. They felt engaged, passionate, and motivated. The beauty for me was that I had not even graded the assignments yet. By employing the guidelines of Universal Design for Learning, I had allowed my students to look at themselves as expert learners—motivated, knowledgeable, and goal oriented. At that moment, the grade was irrelevant. They were all successful!

Universal Design for Learning continues to be a tool I use to inform my pedagogy. I refer to the guidelines consistently, ensuring that the content I offer my students, my teaching strategies, and the assignments through which I assess learning offer multiple means of engagement, representation, and action and expression. Yes, there are days when I spend hours searching through articles, videos, podcasts, blogs, and images to make sure that all students are engaged and can access the content in ways that are meaningful to them. I continue to offer choices, when relevant, in the ways that students can demonstrate their learning. I continue to make sure that content, teaching strategies, and assessments are aligned with the course outcomes. I continue to be transparent about my expectations, providing guidelines, clear rubrics, and samples of assignments. And most importantly, my students continue to be engaged, passionate, motivated, and goal oriented.

How I Got Here

Michelle Dent

My professional career path has followed what you might call a circuitous route. My undergraduate degree is in Spanish and English literature, and while at the time I hoped to teach college Spanish, I quickly realized that not being a native speaker would make this dream very difficult to realize. After college, I landed a job at a Colombian bank in New York City as a receptionist and latched on to my "other dream"—living and working in the Big Apple! I spent the next 12 years immersed in the world of international banking, gaining knowledge and skills by taking continuing education courses and eventually getting my master's degree in business administration. What I learned about myself during those years was that my passion was not just about teaching—it was about learning. While I struggled through many of my business courses (to this day I hyperventilate when someone mentions micro- and macro-economics), I loved going to class, listening to lectures, studying, and applying what I was learning outside of the classroom.

At some point, for reasons not important here, I decided to switch gears and focus on my original dream: to teach. However, at this time in my life, I chose a different direction and returned to college for my master's degree in early childhood education. I found myself in classes that were engaging, and I was surrounded by professors and classmates that were inspirational. Many of my peers were already teaching, and I was in awe of the positive impact they were having on the lives of the children in their classrooms. My passion for teaching was reignited.

My first job in my new career was as a general education teacher in an inclusive kindergarten class of 23. It was exciting, frightening, overwhelming, and exactly where I was meant to be. I gave those

23 children 110% of my energy and employed every one of the strategies I had been taught to support them to meet all of the developmental goals for kindergarteners. Of course, there were days that I felt I had fallen short, so I continued to attend workshops and other professional development opportunities to improve my efforts. After all, I knew that continuing my own educational journey would help me to better support my students. During the years I taught kindergarten and first grade in public school and then owned a childcare center, I continued to study and attend workshops in order to improve my knowledge and skills. My passion for learning never waned.

Finally, 32-and-a-half years after I graduated with my undergraduate degree, I began my career in higher education as a college faculty member teaching young professionals in the field of early childhood education. My training in pedagogy and my years of experience teaching and supporting young children translated successfully into the college classroom. I hoped to motivate and inspire new teachers as I had been motivated and inspired when I studied early childhood education all those years ago.

I am currently taking a course in adult learning theory. It has been exciting because it has introduced me to so many topics that complement my UDL training, from theory to brain research to the myth of learning styles, as well as to strategies for engaging adult learners. I have not lost my passion for learning, or perhaps I should say that I continue to learn in order to stay passionate and motivated and keep my eye on the goal: to teach my students to be high-quality early childhood educators and, perhaps more importantly, expert learners.

Michelle received a bachelor of arts in Spanish from SUNY Albany, a master of business administration from New York University, and a master of science in education from Fordham University. Michelle is a consulting editor for the NAEYC publication Young Children. Her most recent presentations of note include a presentation at the Connecticut Association for the Education of Young Children Annual Conference titled "What Multilingual Learners CAN Do" and a presentation at the fifth annual CAST UDL Symposium titled "Using Learning Goals to Inform Assessment Design." Michelle continues to work toward increasing student engagement, especially in online courses. Her next UDL challenge involves helping students to see themselves as expert learners who are purposeful and motivated, resourceful and knowledgeable, and strategic and goal directed.

Chapter 15

Lisa Coolidge Manley

Transforming Master's Courses Through the Empowerment of Learners

As the director of online studies and an instructional designer for Goodwin University, I have worked on various courses alongside the program director for the Master's of Science in Organizational Leadership (MSOL). We made adjustments as needed to help the cohorts in this degree program succeed, but there were some areas that students were always struggling with. One such barrier was close to my heart: the ability to write more critically. The students also had difficulties with the portfolio process and the order of the courses. As the program director and I continued our exploration of how to foster student achievement, we decided the best way to make change happen was to ask the students what they would change and why. So began the transformation of the Organizational Change Management course's final assignment.

The initial assignment in Organizational Change Management presented students with three documented company issues and asked the students to choose one and to write a change management plan that would address the issue. Students were given the option to work individually or in groups and were asked to write or present orally their change management results. They were asked to think about the information they learned, not only in the course itself, but in previous courses in the program. They were also asked to support their ideas and decisions with sources.

Students presented finished projects that hit each area of the rubric, but many lacked in-depth analysis as to why the changes should take place and how these changes would benefit the companies. One of the learning barriers for these master's students was their ability to fully engage themselves in the assignment. Students could not relate to the company issue they were trying to change. Since they could not relate to the problem, they had no real investment in articulating a solution. The assignment did not enable the students to connect their learning inside the classroom with any real-world and relevant experiences outside the classroom. Other barriers included how the material was offered to students and the timeline given for students to complete the assignment. Originally, a list of requirements was given in the fifth week of the course, allowing the individual or group only two weeks to research, create, and report the findings of their change plans.

My first step was to explore the barriers to better understand how to break them down and create a solution for learners to become more successful. To engage students, it is necessary to provide them with options for pursuing relevance and authenticity, for managing their time, and for fostering collaboration and community (Novak & Rodriguez, 2018). It was important to allow the students time to reflect on their learning experience in the program to determine what has worked for them and what has not. The result was to give them a choice. For those who find autonomy more useful to their work strategies, they were given the option to work on a project individually. For those who work better in a collaborative community, they were given the choice to work in a group setting.

To create better buy-in to the work I was asking students to complete, I had to give them a more relevant problem (or problems) that they could wrap their heads around. Since the program director and I were assessing the MSOL program overall, we quickly decided that it would make sense to allow the students in the program a chance to reflect on and assess their experiences in the program and to create a change plan for the program itself. This challenge could give them an opportunity to have an authentic impact, not only on the development of the MSOL program, but also on their own education and that of the students who come after them.

To create a more active learning strategy, the new change plan was broken down into sections and was scaffolded into four weeks instead of the initial two. The sections of the change plan were articulated in a series of six steps:

Step 1. Demonstrate the reason(s) for the change.

Step 2. Determine and explain the scope of the change.

Step 3. Identify the stakeholders impacted and consider who should be on the team to make this change happen.

Step 4. Clarify the expected benefits of the change.

Step 5. Create a series of milestones that are needed to assure the change is going as expected.

Step 6. Create a change management communication plan.

Scaffolding is an important tool that can be used to break down content into smaller digestible chunks to help the students build their knowledge and make better connections to previous knowledge. It can also be used as a means to increase student engagement by showcasing the methods used to teach in order to help students be more independent and active learners. By scaffolding this final project, the students were able to develop the skills it takes to learn week by week and were given time to improve their ability to think critically.

Each week students were also given multiple forms of content to learn with. This provided students with the opportunity to learn from the kinds of instructional resources that best fit their comprehension needs. Being able to read shorter or longer articles, watch videos, or read from a textbook helped them find the material they learned best from. Students would engage with the content and then engage in a discussion with the class to help them understand the materials they were receiving before going into their groups or to work as an individual developing each step of their plan. Students were also given the opportunity to reach out to their instructor at any stage to ask further questions. Each week, students were also assigned discussion board questions to help them build on their knowledge of the topic for the week and were asked to respond to their peers to promote meaningful learning.

The project gave the students these elements to consider for change:

- Enrollment

- Orientation

- Course alignment

- Course order

- Course layout

- Course discussion board

- Capstone: execution and preparation

- Topics covered in any course

Students were also given options of action and expression to support their planning and development. They were able to choose the format they preferred to use for communicating their proposals to their instructor and peers.

The first semester of this new change plan was astonishing. Creating an assignment that they could relate to empowered them to speak out and become true change agents. The many topics they explored opened my eyes as an instructor and instructional designer about how to transform courses and elements of a course or program to put the learners in control of their educational path.

One of the change plan topics that resonated with me was the discussion board. Many students felt that this type of assignment, which is offered in every course, was little more than a check-off-the-box or a fill-in-the-blank kind of activity. These discussion boards did not seem to have a true connection to student learning. With this final project, several of the groups presented different strategies for designing discussion boards that were more stimulating. Their suggestions proved intriguing enough to become incorporated into the actual MSOL program.

The revised discussion board assignments offered students a two-week window to create their initial post. Instead of a conventional discussion board regimen, where students respond to a new discussion board thread every week, the new arrangement gave students one week to process the course content and then a second week to participate in the discussion board. Waiting until week two to respond to their peers allowed students to make connections between what they learned in week one and the new knowledge the students obtained in week two, enhancing what would have been their week-one response. This schedule also allowed time for students to engage in their own critical thinking. The third week was called "Your turn to drive." In this week, students formulated their own thoughts and questions from the previous weeks. They followed that up with the next week of responses to their peers' questions in a way that mirrored the scaffolding of the prior two weeks. Also, during each post and response, learners were asked to support their work with formal citations. The depth of the posts and responses was thought provoking, dynamic, and meaningful. One of the obstacles students had to overcome was the change in the discussion board format. They were so used to the same old question-and-answer or fill-in-the-blank discussions every week that they found the first two weeks a bit confusing. Once they hit week three and had the freedom to choose their own questions, however, they embraced the change and posted with higher-level thinking. After that semester, I created a short video to explain the expectations of the new discussion board format. This alleviated the anxieties the new cohort might have felt with the changes to the assignment. The new format has facilitated the most engaging discussion boards I have ever seen.

Four semesters have passed by with many of the new change plan ideas implemented. Other courses in the MSOL program were restructured and reordered to create a more cohesive alignment, which made stronger connections to learning for the students. Group projects were added to many of the courses to create a collaborative community of learners. Writing tutors, embedded librarians, and peer-to-peer reviews were added to help learners improve their writing, formatting, and critical thinking skills. Video expectations have been embedded in each week of the course to keep students engaged and to invite instructors to introduce themselves to future students so they are prepared to transition more successfully to the next class.

I am constantly amazed by the knowledge I gain from the students I encounter and the opportunities for growth and empowerment that UDL-based reforms have fostered in our learning environments. I have always been a person who soared when given a vision and the power to create my own learning path. As an instructional designer, I have utilized UDL to create multiple means of engagement for a diverse student population, but as an instructor, I have also seen the capability of UDL to empower students to be active learners who can coordinate their own educational journeys.

How I Got Here

Lisa Coolidge Manley

Looking back on my younger years in K–12, I find myself reflecting on challenges I faced in learning and the disconnect I felt because I did not understand why learning certain subjects like humanities and sciences was so difficult for me and why I could grasp other areas such as computer technology and anything hands on so easily. I realized that when I could not understand the material, I would get easily distracted, and socializing became my way of deflecting. I also found that if I was not engaged in the subject matter, I lost focus. Years later, when I went back to school in my late 20s and early 30s, I found the learning challenges coming back to me. This time, however, I embraced the challenges and explored what was causing them and how I could work through them. I realized I had learning comprehension issues that I had to overcome. It was then that I began to explore the ideas behind Universal Design for Learning for my own academic growth. Visual, auditory, and especially hands-on activities were my top choices for learning.

Reading and writing were difficult for me, and since these skills were so essential to the presentation and assessment of learning in most courses, I was in trouble. By taking a step back, reflecting on, and dissecting where my learning broke down, I realized that one specific area I could work on was building my vocabulary. Being unable to understand the meaning of words made me stumble over the content and caused me to have more anxiety and less ability to build knowledge. As I improved my vocabulary base, my comprehension also began to improve. I found that I became more and more empowered by embracing multiple ways of learning and exploring multiple ways of presenting my knowledge. I was drawn to courses that were more hands on and project based. I also began to understand the importance of communication and that writing was a critical component to learning.

My first career path was in the media communication field. I learned how to write scripts to tell a story and then put the story to video for a wide range of audiences. During this time, I was told by many that I was a good teacher who could explain concepts and demonstrate skills effectively, and that I should consider becoming an educator. Thus, my educational path continued, leading me to receive first my master's in educational technology and then a PhD in education with a focus on instructional design for online learning.

When I began my PhD program in instructional design for online learning, I found myself in new territory. I had never taken an online class before and felt there were a lot of barriers to my learning. I felt like I was back in the early days of my academic career. In the past, I had relied heavily on face-to-face communication to ask questions and receive immediate feedback, and when I did not get it, I felt anxious and began to question my ability to learn all over again. The first course was quite difficult, and even my instructor told me it may not be the right path for my learning. But I am not a quitter, so I pushed on. I broke down my barriers again and began to embrace the platform of online learning. I learned how to expand the confines of the internet walls, and I completed my degree to move into my next career path.

This brings me to today and how I have adopted Universal Design for Learning to empower my students and the institution I work for. Goodwin University has embraced UDL and has offered the faculty opportunities to learn the what, why, and how of implementing UDL. Although I was using bits of UDL in my earlier teaching and designing, I acquired a deeper understanding of the theory and practices as well as the importance of breaking down the barriers to empower students to succeed in their educational journey.

Lisa has her PhD in Education: Instructional Design for Online Learning from Capella University. She has presented at conferences around the continent regarding technology, inclusivity, and assessment. Her next UDL challenge will be to create an educational ecosystem that will continue to empower students on their educational journey far beyond their diplomas.

Chapter 16

Sandi Coyne-Gilbert

UDL and the Golden Ticket: Promoting Student Choice in Graduate Education

One of my basic assumptions upon first developing the Master's of Organizational Leadership (MSOL) program at Goodwin University was that graduate programs are typically structured around written assignments. As a result, I anticipated having students write most of their responses to assignments. Cultivating the skill of writing effectively, however, is a particularly difficult task for many students who often feel that this challenge will keep them from being successful in graduate school. At first, I did not think about how this emphasis on written communication could impact students, simply that there was a distinct responsibility to advocate for quality writing at every opportunity. I have also felt that a graduate degree must add value to a student's life and career. I knew if a student could not express themselves fluently in writing, they were less likely to get the chance to prove themselves and become the leaders they were meant to be. I pushed the importance of writing in the MSOL curriculum, reminding myself that it was in the best interests of the students.

At this time, I was given a wonderful opportunity to study Universal Design for Learning. If you asked me at the time, I would have told you that I engaged students, but when I discovered UDL, I realized that I had only scratched the surface of what it really means to meet students where they are. UDL challenged me to consider different strategies for incorporating multiple means of communication and expression into learning. I realized that by prioritizing the centrality of writing in the MSOL coursework, I might be stifling students' own voices in my efforts to help them succeed in their careers. I had to figure out how to integrate writing into the courses in a way that would accommodate what students wanted to say and how they wanted to share their perspectives.

I discovered that despite the fact that I felt I was fairly flexible in my instructional approach, I did not realize how grounded I was in a restrictive set of expectations regarding student work. I anticipated that writing would be the way all grad students would express themselves, and I constructed a classroom design that reflected this belief. When I stopped and realized that I was not giving students any meaningful choices in how they completed their assignments, I knew I had to change. Though I had learned a great deal with UDL, the path forward did not come easily. I began to consider how to implement a UDL-inspired strategy that would provide multiple means of action and expression for students while sustaining the program's focus on encouraging students to improve their writing. The solution did not appear at first, but as I went forward, I began to find ways to integrate UDL into the graduate program.

I began to work first on the foundational course in the program. The Foundations of Leadership course covers influential theories in the study of leadership while also serving to introduce students to the expectations of the graduate program. One of the goals of this class is to encourage students to believe that they can master leadership skills in their own way. This introductory class was an appropriate testing ground where I could begin the process of using UDL to make the course relevant for every student. I decided that I wanted to structure the course in a way that would make it fun and engaging, rather than overly theoretical. Enter the golden ticket. Everyone is familiar with the story of Willy Wonka and the chocolate factory. You remember the golden ticket, right? If you found the golden ticket, you got to go to the chocolate factory. In the MSOL program, we provided each student with a golden ticket at the beginning of each class. The golden ticket allowed a student to replace a writing assignment with another form of assignment. Every student had to complete all the class assignments, but possession of a golden ticket permitted a student to respond to an assignment prompt using a medium of their choice. The student's decision about how to express their response would be based on what made the most sense to that student, whether that involved writing a song and performing it, composing a poem, or producing a Powtoon animation or a video. The most important element of the assignment was that the student, with the guidance of the instructor, made the decision about what to do to meet the objectives of the assignment in their own way. The power of the golden ticket was that it gave students the ability to choose how to respond to the assignment.

Initially, students did not flock to this new option. Many students found that it was simpler to respond to the assignment in writing, but as the course continued, students began to observe that the process of doing these assignments in alternative media was rewarding enough to merit the extra work of preparation. Suddenly, students were exploring new ways to respond to assignments, and they began to value the golden ticket more highly! Students who used the ticket felt that they were charting their own course and that we as instructors had "given them permission" to be more creative. Essentially, students realized that they were determining what they wanted to achieve in their coursework. The "ticket" gave them more freedom. It became clear that students want to express themselves in their own voice in whatever form best expresses their perspective. However, it is often the case that it takes more time to develop and execute an assignment in this personalized way, and this extra pressure can contribute to a student's sense of feeling overwhelmed. For this reason, students often will simply complete an assignment as directed rather than develop a suggested alternative. With an effective system of support from their instructors and classmates, however, students understand that the initial investment of extra time pays dividends as they become more familiar with the tools and skills that allow them to master these new forms of self-expression. Eventually, students begin to feel bored with the lack of diversity in assignments, and the golden ticket becomes a powerful opportunity for students to stretch their learning and explore new ways of communicating their points of view. Students have risen to "the golden ticket challenge" in a number of creative and memorable ways. In the Foundations of Leadership course, student presentations have taken the form of a live performance of an original song, a poem about leadership, and even a video featuring a theme song about leadership. Students who develop these alternative kinds of presentations engage in a process of discovering what works for them and finding their own perspective. When I share these projects with new students, you can almost see these future leaders thinking, "If another student can do that, why can't I?"

The incorporation of the golden ticket into the course design has evolved to encourage students to work closely with faculty to understand the objectives of the assignment and to achieve them in their own ways. Students have designed classroom activities that help them to explore the expectations of the assignments and to brainstorm novel ways of responding to them. The golden ticket option has become so popular that I have considered including multiple golden tickets in each course. At the same time, the MSOL program continues to emphasize traditional writing skills, and regulating the availability of golden tickets has provided us with an easy mechanism for achieving a balance between introducing flexibility into the assignments and still encouraging students to develop their formal writing abilities.

The use of the golden ticket was the beginning of my UDL journey but certainly not the end. The ticket made me, individually, and the MSOL department, as a collective, question where we could begin to use UDL. Faculty need to reflect actively and continuously on the question of what is working and what is not. Faculty shouldn't feel that everything has to change right away, but they should always be considering how to best support the students and themselves. For this reason, I began to use other kinds of "tickets" in my classes: admission tickets and exit statements. The admission ticket allows the instructor to clarify to students the structure of the class, the course objectives, and the instructor's expectations. In the Foundations of Leadership class, the admission ticket asks incoming students to discuss the difference between management and leadership. The students are given five minutes to provide their insights about management and leadership. The faculty member has a chance to look at these forms briefly and then conduct the class in a way that incorporates the prior knowledge students shared in their admission tickets. At the conclusion of each class, the students have five minutes to complete an "unpacking the suitcase" form that asks an "exit" question about management and leadership. The faculty member can then review these forms and make modifications for the next class, allowing for changes to the curriculum to reemphasize anything that did not seem to resonate with the class.

In our MSOL curriculum, UDL offers students and faculty the opportunity not only to discover how they relate to instructional materials but to give form to their own voice and their own views of leadership. An instructional approach that promotes multiple means of action and expression enables students to dig down deeper into the topics they study and helps instructors to design learning environments that resonate more meaningfully with students. My efforts to find ways to make the coursework more intuitive and accessible have led me to focus on the core goals of each class, cutting through the busywork to ensure that every activity that students participate in furthers their learning in a genuine way that they perceive as worthwhile.

Has UDL improved the quality of our graduate classes? Yes, there is no doubt about it.

Before I was introduced to UDL, I explored various approaches to enhance students' learning experiences, but I had forgotten the elements that really matter. I had not considered strategies for moving beyond merely entertaining students to designing ways of involving them in their own learning. A UDL-based approach also empowers our program's faculty to craft experiences that reinforce the value of intentional, engaging, and authentic leadership. In our classrooms, learning about leadership is not only a course of study; it is a way of life that begins when students make their own executive decisions about their own learning process in a way that unleashes their inner voice and taps into their passion about their work. As I move forward with the MSOL program, UDL will continue to play an integral role in its educational philosophy.

How I Got Here

Sandi Coyne-Gilbert

I often say that I came to teaching in a backdoor sort of way. I never set out to be a college professor. I was a single mom with two children, and I wanted an education. I felt that if I could get a bachelor's and a master's degree, I could earn an income that would support my family in a loving and comfortable style. I had an advisor in my master's program, however, who had other plans for me. He was incredible. He would spend time with my kids if they had a snow day, and they grew to really like him. He was a wonderful man and a true advisor who wanted to influence my path. Toward the end of my MBA, he approached me and asked if I wanted to teach a class. I told him firmly that I never wanted to teach. He asked if I had ever taught before, and I replied that I had no teaching experience but that I knew I wouldn't like it. He pushed on, saying, "Look, I took care of your kids so you could go to class. You owe me." I was clearly stuck, and so I agreed. Later, he told me he saw "it" in me; he knew I was meant to teach, and he was not going to let me shirk my destiny. I was about five minutes into teaching my first class when I realized that teaching was exactly what I wanted to do with my life.

After that critical experience, I began to accept teaching positions here and there and eventually became a full-time professor at Springfield College in Springfield, Massachusetts. I developed my own teaching style, and then I began to explore strategies for improving my teaching approach to reach more students and to have a greater impact. I am now the program director of a leadership program built on the principle that everyone can discover leadership skills within themselves. At Goodwin University, I discovered that developing an academic program intended to help students discover their own "inner leader" provided a perfect opportunity for me to continue to reflect on my own teaching practice.

Sandi received a bachelor of science in business and an MBA in health care from Western New England University, and she earned a doctor of management in organizational leadership from University of Phoenix. Sandi continues to explore topics related to leadership that help students move their careers forward. Some of her favorite topics include personal branding, crisis leadership, and imposter syndrome. Sandi's current UDL challenge is to create a more strategic and impactful experience for the Master's in Organizational Leadership students surrounding their portfolios; she believes UDL offers insights for the faculty to restructure the portfolio process.

Afterword:
The UDL Transformation

Nicole Brewer

The UDL stories collected in this book illustrate the transformative nature of education. We write not only about the transformations in our classrooms and students but also about ourselves. Simply put, UDL has changed us. We think differently. And this different way of thinking has changed our teaching and, more broadly, has changed our institution.

What makes our experience at Goodwin unique is that we have been on this journey of transformation together. We have been given a rare opportunity to develop a community of practice that expands across the entire university. Our community of practice is a group of faculty who are dedicated to supporting and uplifting our students. That dedication has led to ongoing, enthusiastic, and invigorating conversations about what it means to cultivate a learning environment that benefits all our students.

I am truly inspired by the work my colleagues do. Since so many of us are committed to learning and growing together, I have had the pleasure of seeing UDL in action. I have seen students laugh while they learn with their classmates, make breakthroughs in their understanding, and feel empowered when they successfully communicate all they have learned. My colleagues are creating an atmosphere that allows their students to recognize their own potential and feel confident enough to strive to reach that potential.

While we hope our stories give you new insights about how to reduce barriers in the learning environment for your students, this book is also about building community in higher education. It is about how our decision to learn together has had a real and positive impact on our students. This book is an invitation for you to join us on this UDL journey. Whether you are new to UDL or you are an expert, we ask you to see yourself as part of a larger community of educators by developing your own local community of practice. A community like this can change you. It can transform you, it can transform your institution, and most importantly, it can transform your students.

Further Reading

UDL University is a book of stories about how postsecondary teachers have implemented UDL principles in their classrooms. To learn more about the background of UDL and the science behind it, we recommend the following books:

- *Universal Design for Learning: Theory and Practice* by Anne Meyer, David H. Rose, and David Gordon (2014, CAST)

- *UDL Now! A Teacher's Guide to Applying Universal Design for Learning in Today's Classrooms* by Katie Novak (2016, CAST)

- *Engage the Brain: How to Design for Learning That Taps Into the Power of Emotion* by Allison Posey (2019, ASCD)

- *Unlearning: Changing Your Beliefs and Your Classroom With UDL* by Allison Posey and Katie Novak (2020, CAST)

- *UDL Navigators in Higher Education: A Field Guide* by Jodie Black and Eric J. Moore (2019, CAST)

- *Equity by Design: Delivering on the Promise and Power of UDL* by Mirko Chardin and Katie Novak (2020, Corwin Press)

▮ *Antiracism and Universal Design for Learning: Building Expressways to Success* by Andratesha Fitzgerald (2020, CAST)

▮ *Reach Everyone, Teach Everyone: Universal Design for Learning in Higher Education* by Thomas J. Tobin and Kirsten T. Behling (2018, West Virginia University Press)

References

Bell, L. A. (2007). Theoretical foundations for social justice. In M. Adams, L. A. Bell, & P. Griffin (Eds.), *Teaching for Diversity and Social Justice* (pp. 1–16). Routledge.

Carroll, K. (2012, July). *Play is necessary* [Video]. TEDxHarlem Talk. *https://www.youtube.com/watch?v=1pz72Wygg8c*

CAST. (n.d.). *About UDL*. *http://udloncampus.cast.org/page/udl_about*

CAST. (2018). *Universal Design for Learning Guidelines version 2.2*. *http://udlguidelines.cast.org*

Klopfer, E., Osterweil, S., and Salen, K. (2009). *Moving learning games forward: Obstacles, opportunities, and openness*. Education Arcade. *https://education.mit.edu/wp-content/uploads/2018/10/Moving-LearningGamesForward_EdArcade.pdf*

Meyer, A., Rose, D. H., & Gordon, D. (2014). *Universal Design for Learning: Theory and practice*. CAST Professional Publishing.

Novak, K., & Rodriguez, K. (2018). *UDL progression rubric*. CAST. *http//castpublishing.org/novak-rodriquez-udl-progression-rubric/*

Ralabate, P. K. (2011). Universal Design for Learning: Meeting the needs of all students. *The ASHA Leader, 16*(10). *https://doi.org/10.1044/leader.FTR2.16102011.14*

Taddei, L. M., & Budhai, S. S. (2017). *Nurturing young innovators: Cultivating creativity in the classroom, home, and community*. International Society for Technology in Education.

The Art of Concise Presentations. (2019). *https://medium.com/digital-society/pechakucha-55ffaaa2b1/*

Index

"What is good for some is good
    for all," 113–114
writing versus publication, 114
composition: revision
    barriers to learning, 96–97
    giving and receiving feedback, 97
    interpersonal communication, 97
    peer review strategies, 97–99
    revision, 95–101
    social connections, 100
    student preferences, 95–96
    student-centered solutions,
        99–100
    writing for communication and
        thinking, 102
comprehension, facilitating, 55
computer applications
    breaking up units, 32
    choice and autonomy, 32–33
    cracking passwords, 34
    incorporating questions, 33
    maintaining student attention, 33
    minimizing threats and
        distractions, 32
    Nearpod app, 32–35
    PowerPoints, 31–32
    presentation of material, 32
    reflection, 32
    relevance, value, and
        authenticity, 32
    SMART Board, 33, 35
    speech anxiety, 54
    student engagement, 32
    UDL-improved presentation, 35
    virtual field trips, 33–34
    websites, 34
confidence builder, UDL as, 26
connecting, with why, 14–15
connections
    making, 9–17, 53–54
    passion for, 16–17
consistency, increasing, 23
conversations with students,
    engaging in, 11
Coolidge Manley, Lisa, 161–170
course flexibility, 124

Coyne-Gilbert, Sandi, 171–179
curriculum development, 19–20

D

Dent, Michelle, 151–160
didactic and laboratory components,
    connecting, 10
discussion boards, 53–62
diversity of learners, anticipating, 2
drafting (composition)
    group activities, 87
    ideas for essays, 87–88
    identifying main goal, 88
    introducing ideas to
        audiences, 86
    introduction paragraph, 85–89
    lecture less, engage more, 86
    student preferences, 89
    visual and auditory
        introductions, 87
    and visual media, 86

E

ECE (early childhood education)
    American Academy of
        Pediatrics, 154
    assessing student success, 151–157
    building safe space for risk,
        144–145
    collaboration, 143–147
    Education and Technology,
        141–147
    games and play, 143–147
    Kahoot!, 145–147
    National Association for the
        Education of Young
        Children, 154
    outcomes for assessment, 153
    revised assignment, 155
    revised rubric, 156
    risk-taking and failure, 141
    school readiness assignment, 154
    Spanish-speaking students, 155–157
    student perspectives, 154–155
    student reflection, 157
    support for writing, 152–157

Index